Also by Helen Ruttencutter:

PIANIST'S PROGRESS
QUARTET

Previn

by

Helen Ruttencutter

MICHAEL JOSEPH
LONDON

First published in Great Britain by Michael Joseph Ltd
44 Bedford Square, London WC1
1985

British Library Cataloguing in Publication Data
Ruttencutter, Helen
  Previn.
  1. Previn, Andre   2. Conductors (Music) –
  Biography
  I. Title
785'.092'4   ML422.P/

ISBN 0–7181–2402–2

Typeset by Cambrian Typesetters,
Frimley, Surrey
Printed by Hollen Street Press, Slough and bound
by Hunter & Foulis, Edinburgh

Acknowledgments

The author and publishers would like
to thank the following for
permission to quote extracts:
the *Daily Telegraph* (Anthony Payne);
The Times ('Four Ages of a musician
for All Seasons' by Norman Lebrecht)
and the *Guardian* (Michael John White).

To William Shawn

LIST OF ILLUSTRATIONS

In between pages 120 & 121

Part I

CHAPTER 1

To André Previn, one of the most pleasing sounds in the world is that of an orchestra tuning, and when the orchestra is the Pittsburgh Symphony, of which he is the music director, the pleasure is enhanced. Previn, like other music directors of major symphony orchestras in America, spends comparatively little time with his orchestra – fourteen weeks, September through May, at three- or four-week intervals, plus two or three weeks on domestic or European tour, with carefully chosen guest conductors filling in the gaps of a fifty-two-week season. The rest of the year, using a twenty-acre country home in Surrey as his base, he is the guest conductor of all the major symphony orchestras in the Western world.

Previn likes to get to Pittsburgh forty-eight hours before the first rehearsal for a concert. He takes the Concorde – it not only saves time, he says, but 'cuts down on cowardice' – and one day late in April in 1980, he went to Heathrow Airport only to be told that the flight had been cancelled and he should come back the following day. So he arrived in Pittsburgh late and irritated. Also, he had a cold. His first stop at Heinz Hall, the home of the Pittsburgh Symphony, at nine-thirty on the morning of the first rehearsal, was Dinah Daniels's office. Miss Daniels, who was the Pittsburgh Symphony's director of public relations, is a tall, attractive young woman with hazel eyes, short, wavy reddish-blond hair, and a trim figure, kept trim by half a dozen trips a day from her office, on the third floor in the front of the building, to the backstage, on the first floor at the rear. She is a cheerful, intelligent woman with uncommon common sense, and a sense of humour, too. Previn greeted her, as he does all women friends, with a kiss on each cheek, a gesture that is

3

ingratiating, and also serves the purpose of keeping the recipient at arm's length. Miss Daniels's laugh has the sound of a Swiss bell, and when Previn, in duffel coat, jeans, fisherman's cap, and ankle-high black boots, told her about the delayed flight – elaborating on the inconvenience of trying to save three and a half hours and losing twenty-four – she laughed. It seemed to cheer him up, and he laughed too. Previn's face is an interesting one: the nose prominent, the mouth sensuous, the planes of his face hardly visible, the eyes, behind wide-rimmed black-framed glasses, blue. His hair is black but turning grey, and it frames his face in a modified Beatles cut. In repose, his face is expressionless. His friends know him to be a witty man, but when he is told a joke or an anecdote he seems to be pondering the different levels, anticipating the destination, the punch line. He may nod approval. But when he is surprised, his face goes into action – eyes crinkle shut, mouth turns up, opens, head goes back, and he gasps with laughter. His friend Adolph Green says, 'André's sense of nonsense is as great as that of anyone I know. His is a Perelman-Benchley world. He's constantly amused at the absurdity of life, the foolishness of people's behaviour. It's not easy to make him actually laugh, but it's a pleasure. He becomes absolutely *crippled* with laughter.'

Miss Daniels's office, in addition to a desk, a typewriter, and a few chairs, had a deep-blue Oriental rug; a five-foot-two papier-mâché musician in white tie and tails in one corner; framed posters stamped 'Sold Out' of Pittsburgh Symphony concerts at Avery Fisher Hall; a framed Carnegie Hall Ninetieth Anniversary poster; and a big food stamp with Previn's picture in the middle, which someone in the office had printed (a hint that the salaries weren't what they should be). That day, her desk held a pile of letters, requests, appeals – matters that required a decision from Previn. He glanced at the stack and said, 'I should do what Lenny does – A and C, accept and cancel.' (Lenny is, of course, Leonard Bernstein.) Two matters demanded immediate attention. The following week, auditions would be held to fill the principal-second-violin chair – the current occupant was retiring – and someone from the *New York Times* wanted to observe. Previn said, 'No, no, no! These things are tough enough as it is.' The second request was an invitation to the Pittsburgh to play at Resorts International Hotel, in Atlantic City. As a matter of fact, an account in the *New York Times* said that Previn and the Pittsburgh, the Boston Symphony Orchestra, with Seiji Ozawa, and the New York Philharmonic, with Zubin Mehta, were all going to give concerts there. Previn said, 'Absolutely not.' (Ozawa also refused, but Mehta accepted.) Miss Daniels then told him that the morning and afternoon rehearsals would be held in Heinz Hall's big practice room, on the fourth floor; Gulf Oil had taken over the auditorium for its annual shareholders' meeting. Previn said, 'I *hate* that big phone booth. The acoustics are *atrocious.*' Previn's career spans two venues (four, if you include Hollywood and jazz), and his speech reflects this. With total inconsistency, he says 'concertos' and 'concerti', 'tempos' and 'tempi', 'interval' and 'intermission'. 'Tune', for theme or melody, is English, and he bites his tongue to keep from saying 'semiquaver' for sixteenth note when he's in America. A soft-spoken man whose voice has the timbre of an oboe, Previn often speaks in italics to get his message across. Nevertheless, he's a pro at bowing to the inevitable, like Gulf Oil, and, saying 'I'll see you later', he headed for the rehearsal.

Whenever Previn returns to Pittsburgh, he deliberately schedules a programme that is tough for the orchestra. He feels they're never in quite the same shape they were in when he left them, and that a difficult piece will force them to play better immediately. On one occasion it was the Berlioz Requiem, which he calls 'World War III'. This time, it would be the Rachmaninoff Symphony No. 3 – every bit as difficult as the same composer's legendary third piano concerto – and the Brahms second piano concerto, with one of Previn's favourite pianists, the Cuban-born Horacio Gutiérrez. Gutiérrez would not arrive until Thursday morning, the day of the first concert, so Previn had Tuesday and Wednesday to work with the orchestra. He decided on a string rehearsal in the morning, and brass, woodwinds, and percussion in the afternoon. In Rachmaninoff, brass and woodwinds can cover a multitude of sins in the string section, and there would be no hiding this morning.

The big practice room has an eighteen-foot ceiling, and the white walls are covered with inverted-shield-shaped white panels that could certainly cause sound to ricochet. The violins, violas, cellos, and basses were there, practising and chattering, when Previn came in, at ten. He threaded his way through them, pausing to say hello to several players, and then, seated on a high stool on the podium, he said to everyone: 'Nice to see you again.' Orchestra members applaud one another by shuffling their feet, and they did this now for Previn.

Previn smiled acknowledgment and said, 'Before we start the Rachmaninoff, whatever markings you have, they're not mine.' He said to Fritz Siegal, his leader, who, in the absence of an oboe had just given an A for the others to tune to, 'In Vienna, they tune to *four fifty*.' Most American orchestras prefer the lower-pitched 440 A. Siegal, a slight man with brown hair, a trim moustache and beard, and blue eyes, looked amused. (New music directors usually choose their own leader, but Siegal was with the Pittsburgh when Previn arrived, and Previn counts it a blessing that Siegal is there. He says that in addition to being an excellent leader and a supreme soloist Siegal is 'very funny, *witty*, sometimes a rake, but he doesn't show that to strangers', and he adds, 'Sometimes visiting conductors don't find out.')

The rehearsal was nerve-racking. The players all sounded terrible – ragged and insecure. Many were sight-reading a work that was unfamiliar to them. It isn't programmed often, and it hadn't been played in Pittsburgh in over forty years. Previn said, 'You're not watching the hairpins.' 'Hairpins' is a musicians' term for crescendo and diminuendo markings. 'If you don't, the winds, who follow, will be in trouble.' Previn works up quite a head of steam when he conducts, and his usually pale face was flushed. As the strings played, he said, 'Watch what comes at Forty-seven. It's pretty funny.' And then, 'Stay *ironclad* in your rhythm. Once we get everyone cooking on that, it's really vicious.' The clarinettist Gervase de Peyer, who was in the London Symphony Orchestra for a number of years, has offered an explanation of why Previn lasted so long with that independent, self-governed orchestra – an unprecedented eleven and a half years: 'He's got a way with him, André. With all orchestras there are difficult moments, and he's very good at using the moment for a witty, amusing remark that puts things in perspective.') Now there was a terrible tangle, and Previn said, 'Was anyone hurt in that wreck?' He laughed at a messy pizzicato passage in the cello section, and said, 'Stay out of this. You're only confusing us.' There were groans and gripes from all directions. During a pause, a violinist muttered, 'I feel like I'm walking on eggshells.' Previn heard it, and said, 'I picked this with malice aforethought.' He zeroed in on a theme that started with the firsts, was picked up by the seconds, passed to the violas, and then on to the cellos and basses – fast and delicate and completely exposed. Previn said, 'I've only done this piece once before – years ago. That spot is trouble. The critics will blast us for that passage alone. When more awkward string parts are written, I don't want to see them.' It's atypical of him to be negative, and now he smiled and said, 'Nevertheless, we're stuck with it, so let's do it right.' He called a tricky cello passage 'the musicians'-union entrance test', and told the cellos, 'You don't get any help from anybody on those four bars, so it has to be *exactly* right. After that, we're back in Rach land, and it's not so bad.'

7

As the rehearsal progressed, the sound improved, and Previn looked relieved. At twelve-thirty on the dot, Aaron Chaifetz, watch in hand, viola under arm, rose and approached the podium. A huge, jolly man, he seems to loom as he walks. He is the personnel manager, and the watch is the signal that time's up – union rules. Previn always keeps the left cuff of any shirt he's wearing – red-and-white checked cotton today – unbuttoned for easy access to *his* watch, and he has usually finished what he'd planned to do by the time Chaifetz looms. Previn thanked the musicians and said he would see them the following morning.

Previn's quarters, an office with dressing room, closet, and bathroom, are off the street stage-door entrance, past the greenroom, and down a long corridor, behind the stage proper. His office is furnished with a large black-leather-topped desk, a sofa covered in a tan-and-brown print, and an assortment of chairs. Previn made only a few changes in his quarters when he took over from his predecessor, William Steinberg; he added a small refrigerator in a corner, and he removed two etchings of Bruckner. Bruckner is a composer Previn has yet to conduct. He says, 'I like religious music, but I can't stand his piety. I wish he would get up off his knees.' In place of the etchings are two framed crayon drawings done by his son Matthew: one is of a brown-suited conductor wearing a black bow tie and holding his baton pointed skyward, and is signed, with many Xs, 'Matthew, 1978'; the other is made up of black figures representing a symphony orchestra, with all the players in the proper places, and is signed 'To Papa, with love. Matthew, October 27, 1978.' Also on the walls are score pages that Previn has had mounted and framed in black: a page from the Schubert C-Major Quintet; a page from Britten's 'War Requiem'.

Waiting in Previn's office after the rehearsal was Sid Kaplan. A handsome man of medium height, with grey hair and an open, pleasant manner, Kaplan was for many years a French-horn player in the Pittsburgh Symphony.

Then he quit, moved to Ohio and went into business. But he missed the music world, and when the business failed he returned to the orchestra, and eventually became its manager. He is a good friend of Previn's, and is almost paternally protective of him. His staff keeps the refrigerator in Previn's office stocked with fruit juice and yogurt, and he also makes sure that there is food in Previn's apartment when he returns to Pittsburgh. In addition, Kaplan sometimes drives Previn to and from engagements. Dinah Daniels was there, too.

Previn calls Kaplan Kap or Kappy, and now he said, 'Kap, I promised Gary Graffman I would listen to his star pupil today. I can hear her practising on that god-awful piano in the greenroom. Can you find something better for her?' Previn paused, and added, 'It's so terrible she'd be better off with an accordion.' Another pause, and then he laughed. 'Maybe she sings.' Previn was skipping his lunch hour to hear the pupil, Lydia Artymiw. Previn likes to encourage young musicians, but finds it hard to pass judgment on them. Once, he and Vladimir Ashkenazy, who are good friends, were in the same city. Musicians' paths cross in odd places, like the routes on boastful airline maps, and on this occasion Previn and Ashkenazy and Itzhak Perlman were all in Daytona Beach, Florida. Ashkenazy had agreed to listen to a young pianist there and advise her honestly about whether she had any chance of a career as a concert pianist. He invited Previn to come along and listen. Previn went, though he hated to do so, and chose an inconspicuous seat at the back of the room. Ashkenazy had to discourage her. She pleaded with him. If she practised eight hours a day, got a different teacher. . . And he had to tell her, 'Not in a million years. You can play for your own pleasure, for your friends, chamber music. But a career – no.' I hoped Miss Artymiw would be good.

Miss Daniels brought a sandwich and a Coke to Previn's office, and he returned from the audition looking pleased. Miss Artymiw had, it turned out, decided to stick with the

9

piano she'd been practising on, and Previn said, 'That girl is *fabulous*! What a technique! Even on that terrible piano. There isn't *anything* she can't play. Fantastic!' Concerts are planned and soloists booked well in advance. Miss Artymiw was booked to play with the Pittsburgh three seasons later.

The brass, woodwind, and percussion rehearsal was handled almost with dispatch. Often, given the sheer number of notes the strings play, and the numbers in each section – seventeen first violins, fifteen seconds, twelve violas, eleven cellos, and nine basses in the Pittsburgh – it seems that getting them to sound good together is more than half the battle with any orchestra. Previn did single out the first oboe, Elden Gatwood. He said, 'Elden, I think it's absolutely wonderful that you *never* have to breathe, but in that long solo you could sneak a breath in, just before F, if you want to.'

And then Previn met with management, on the fifth floor – something he looks forward to every bit as much as a visit to the dentist. Programmes, personnel problems, recording sessions, whether or not to buy a new piano must all be 'talked into the ground', and there's always a certain amount of bureaucratic red tape involved. Previn sighs with relief when the session is over.

Several years ago, Previn formed a piano trio with Herbert Greenberg, the associate leader, and Anne Martindale Williams, the principal cellist. At first, they played just for their own pleasure, but in 1979 they gave a concert at the local YMCA, as part of the Y's chamber-music series. According to Stephen Dick, who produced the 'Previn and the Pittsburgh' broadcasts for public television, 'the audience applauded and stamped their feet, and if they'd had flowers they would have thrown them.' This season, the trio was scheduled to play at the Y Music Society the following Tuesday, and again a week later. Formidable programmes: Beethoven's monumental 'Archduke' and the Ravel Trio the first Tuesday, and the Beethoven 'Ghost' Trio and the Brahms B-Major the following week. In this busy time, Previn fitted trio rehearsals in whenever he could. Also, in two weeks, when Itzhak Perlman would be the soloist in two concertos – the Korngold and the Conus, both of which would also be recorded after the concerts were over – a jazz recording session was planned. Previn and Perlman had recorded some Scott Joplin, at Perlman's request. Previn felt the peak of the Joplin craze had passed, but he did it nevertheless. The record turned out to be one of Perlman's bestsellers, and now he wanted to record some jazz. This week, Previn planned to write eight original tunes for his friend, so that Perlman would not be compared by critics with legitimate jazz violinists, and, in order to make the record as good as it could possibly be, he was flying in to Pittsburgh Shelly Manne, from Los Angeles, on drums; Jim Hall, from New York ('an absolute *genius*'), on guitar; and Red Mitchell, from Stockholm, on bass. Previn had worked with all of them in the fifties, when he was active – and acclaimed – as a jazz pianist. One of the bestselling jazz records of all time was a 1956 recording of 'My Fair Lady' by Shelly Manne and Friends, one of whom was Previn. Also in the fifties, Manne played drums in the André Previn Trio.

This afternoon, after the meeting with management, Previn, Greenberg, and Mrs Williams got together in the big practice room and tore into the Ravel. Before they started, Mrs Williams asked Previn if he had practised.

Previn said, 'Are you kidding? With this piece? You're damned right I did.'

Mrs Williams is a petite young woman with blue eyes, golden hair, and a ready tendency to blush. Greenberg is of medium height and has a mop of curly brown hair that almost hides his features. He is given to wearing jeans and running shoes and a Pittsburgh Pirates T-shirt. He and Previn are friends, and Previn often goes to the Greenbergs' for dinner and games of Scrabble. Greenberg was currently giving serious thought to moving to a lesser orchestra, where he could be leader rather than just associate. Siegal was a youthful sixty-two, and Previn hoped he would stay on well beyond the optional retirement age of sixty-five. Even though Previn let Greenberg play concertos frequently with the symphony, partly in the hope of keeping him there, too, for Greenberg it was still not the same as being Number One.

Many musicians consider the Ravel to be the composer's finest chamber work. Filled with elastic give-and-take rubatos, it is an extremely difficult piece to play. Previn's edition of the score was French, and included explanations of an occasional mystery that the others' Kalmus edition was vague about. Nevertheless, Previn sometimes deferred to Mrs Williams on matters of interpretation – she had studied the work at Curtis with Isidore Cohen, the violinist with the Beaux Arts Trio. They made their way through the first movement, pausing to discuss certain points, and then played it through without stopping. After they'd finished, Previn said, 'All the things we didn't talk about were fine. All the things we talked about were *terrible*.' He laughed, and added, 'A depressing thought – we'll be better off if we rely on instinct.' Although they were working hard, they were playing, too, and he paused to say, 'Have you seen Gretchen's metronome?' Gretchen Van Hoesen is the orchestra's principal harp. 'Is that fun! You can set five counter rhythms at the same time, at different volumes and different accents. I had fun with that! I can't tell you.'

Before they began the second movement, Previn played a theme from it and said, 'For me, it's like "La Valse". Any faster than that, and the terror goes, and it becomes a scherzo.' Glancing at Mrs Williams, he said, 'Annie, I can tell by your smile you want it faster.'

Mrs Williams blushed a bit and said, 'No, not really.'

Previn has been accused of favouring young players. In 1978, when Nathaniel Rosen, then the principal cellist, won the Tchaikovsky Competition and left the Pittsburgh, a flock of cellists from all over the country auditioned for his chair. So did Mrs Williams, who had been Rosen's assistant section leader for a couple of years. Previn was criticised for choosing her because of her youth, but his judgment has proved to be wise. She's a strong section leader, and in all the solos that come up in the orchestral literature her sound is warm and lush and her playing eloquent. She said of a theme in the second movement of the Ravel, 'Every time I hear that, I think of cocktail music.'

Previn said, 'Absolutely!' He played it in his best cocktail-music style, and as he played he said, 'Yeah. . . Yeah. . .Sure. . . It's even *harmonised* that way. But he saves it by having all those eighth notes in the cello and violin against it.'

Previn said after they'd played the third movement, at a slow tempo, 'We have to make sure this thing doesn't turn into Delius. I can't believe this tempo, but you're the one who studied it. Incidentally, at Eight, it's not a brand-new thought at all. It's not a paragraph.'

After they'd finished the fourth movement, Greenberg said to Previn, 'What you did before Five was a great idea – it really sets it.'

Previn said, 'Well, it was partly an idea and partly panic. I'm so proud of playing that run – I'm never going to do *that* again.' He glanced at his watch; it was six-thirty. He closed his music and stood up, and the others did the same. Previn said, 'I think we sound terrific. I'd like us to play on one of my BBC shows – maybe next year.' Then he remembered that Greenberg might be leaving Pittsburgh, and he said, 'I'm sorry, Herbie. That was insensitive of me. Look, you can still be in the trio.' He started to laugh, and added, 'But not on camera.' (The trio has not yet played on the BBC, but in February of 1983 they gave a concert in Baltimore's new Joseph Meyerhoff Hall, home of the Baltimore Symphony, of which Greenberg is now the leader.)

13

Previn lives in a neighbourhood with sparse conveniences, and after saying goodbye to Greenberg and Mrs Williams he walked half a block to a takeout delicatessen and bought a roast chicken and 'coleslaw for one'. He took the food back to Heinz Hall, where Kaplan was waiting to drive him home.

On Thursday morning, Previn, who has said he never feels he's really in Pittsburgh until he is in the hall, on the podium, and facing the full orchestra, arrived early for the ten-o'clock rehearsal. The hall, which was renovated in 1970, is a confection of concert-hall colours – red plush seats, red carpets, gold-flecked white wallpaper. The box seats and the grand tier are edged in gold, and have decorative lacy gold medallions along the sides, through which light flickers when the house lights are dimmed. While Previn was backstage talking to Miss Van Hoesen – 'one of *the* greatest in the country,' he says; she looked too young to be the greatest anything just yet – Miss Daniels came down from her office to tell him that the rehearsal would be 'open'.

Previn looked startled, and asked, 'The blue-haired ladies?'

Miss Daniels nodded, and added, 'And children, too.'

'*Children*? How *old*? Oh, God.'

At ten, with the entire orchestra onstage, Previn, seated on a high stool on the podium, had a few words to say to the musicians. With a glance at Chaifetz, he said, 'I don't know if I'm allowed to say this. Tell me, those maroon ties you wear for the Sunday-afternoon concerts – is that a management rule? You look like Roxy ushers.' Applause from the orchestra members. They didn't like them, either. 'Well, get something different – but no jokes.' Someone in the cello section muttered something, and his colleagues laughed. Previn said, 'What was that?' and the cellist said, 'The ladies' – there were sixteen in the Pittsburgh – 'should wear maroon ties and nothing else.'

14

Previn shook his head in disbelief. Then he went on to another subject, treading gently. He isn't accustomed to management or union rules, because of all the conducting he does in Europe. In Pittsburgh, according to Previn, someone is forever saying, 'Yes, but in Section 3, Paragraph B . . .' He said now, 'And something else bothers me. You ought to be sitting on risers. I can't see some of the woodwinds and brass, and I suspect they can't see me, either.' There were dissenting murmurs. Some of the players in the rear had long sections of rests in certain pieces – enough time to read before they had to come in. Previn said, 'Well, I'm sorry. Rules or no rules, you're going to have risers. Makeshift ones for this concert and the rest of the season. During the summer, I'll have some nice ones specially built.'

The piano was in place onstage, to Previn's left. As the hall was filling up, Gutiérrez arrived to rehearse the Brahms. The orchestra members applauded when he came onstage, and Previn hopped down to shake hands and greet him. Gutiérrez, a tall, heavyset, sandy-haired young man, in a grey business suit, acknowledged the applause with a nod and exchanged a few words with Previn. Then he sat down at the piano and, twirling the stool's knobs, adjusted the seat to a height that was comfortable for him. He is shy, almost humble, in demeanour, but is in awesome command once he starts to play. Previn enjoys accompanying soloists, and it is a rare programme that does not include one. He often uses soloists when the orchestra is on tour – something that most music directors tend not to do, since the whole point of a tour is to show off the orchestra itself. Perhaps his rapport with soloists is a result of the fact that when he was in his teens and early twenties he was often the piano soloist himself. His sensitive ear counts, too. Once, Vladimir Ashkenazy rehearsed the Brahms First Concerto with the London Symphony Orchestra. At the end of the rehearsal, Ashkenazy remained onstage, playing the slow movement. When Previn was almost out of earshot, he heard a slight sweetness that had not been there during the rehearsal. He spun around. Ashkenazy was looking at him and grinning. He said, 'I *thought* I could get your attention without shouting at you.'

Before returning to the podium, Previn turned and made an announcement to the audience. 'Today, we don't have time to even be *aware* of you. This is not a dress rehearsal. It's a *first* rehearsal. So, please, no applause.' Then Previn began the Brahms. He can have flu and fever, jet lag and no sleep, but when he conducts he comes to life, radiates energy, wills what he wants. With his left hand he demands, beseeches, cajoles, soothes, quiets; with the hand doubled into a fist, pulled toward him, he is saying, 'More, *more*.' He also cues with his left hand, and Harold Smoliar, the English horn, who in some pieces has lots of time to read, says, almost in wonderment, 'He never lets me down.' Smoliar adds, 'We feed off his adrenaline', to which Previn says, 'That's what I'm here for.' At times, the baton, in Previn's right hand, is pointed toward the ceiling in preparation for a downbeat. Sometimes both arms are raised high, hands curved down: an eagle in flight.

At rehearsal, Previn abandons the stool the moment the music begins. When he stops to correct a spot, he clenches the baton between his teeth to free his hands for score-page turning. Orchestra musicians are compulsive talkers – a release from their tense task. While they're playing, it's almost as if they were thinking up a joke to pass along during the next pause. But Pittsburgh players are attentive enough to require only a 'Sh-h-h, *sh-h-h*', instead of handclaps, from Previn to make them shut up and settle down. Often he will stop and ask 'What was that?' so he can enjoy the joke, too.

He stopped now and then to say something to the orchestra. 'At Letter L, you get too excited. I'd appreciate it if you'd mark that crescendo just piano.' He flipped pages. 'Basses – that great big theme at Letter F. He's playing a brand-new piano. Give him a chance.' More page turnings and several 'Sh-h-h's'. 'Violas, cellos, at K. *Listen* to what's happening. Keep your eyes open – it's not necessarily metronomic.' Then, *'Liberate* the tune a little. Everyone has piano, but it shouldn't all be the same.' They played the phrase and he grinned with pleasure. 'See?' They played on, and were stopped. 'You're *frantically* not together. I don't understand what's hard there.' They backed up and played the same section to his satisfaction. To the strings, 'Now *sing!*' On they went. Then, baton down, 'Sh-h-h, sh-h-h. Forgive me for saying it, but when a passage is awkward, OK. But that was just carelessness.' Once more into the music. 'Oh, that's *nice!*' The seconds had the theme. 'Seconds, are you actually playing that on the D-string?' Someone in the section said, 'It's awkward.' Previn said, 'Just do it the first time; second time around you can change it. I like the colour.' He stopped and flipped pages. 'At M. Try to think of it as a melodic line – put melodic weight on each note.' They played the phrase. 'Now some of you are playing it a little soloistically.' He flipped more pages. 'There's wholesale confusion at O. Everyone is looking personally guilty. I mean *all* of you.' They played the O section. 'Now you sound as if you're *hoping* you're right.' They played it again and then continued into the development section. Previn stopped them. 'Somebody doesn't want to come in on time.' He laughed. 'I can't say it any more tactfully than that.' He watched Gutiérrez closely, smiled when he did something individualistic, or played what Previn knew to be an almost impossible passage flawlessly. During the slow movement, without stopping the orchestra, he left the podium to speak to Elden Gatwood, the oboe. There is a recurring, haunting cello solo in that movement, and on his way back to the podium Previn said to Siegal, 'Isn't Annie *wonderful?*' With an occasional 'More, *more*' at climaxes, or 'Oh, that's *lovely*' of something softer, they completed the last movement.

Chaifetz had left the orchestra and was standing near the stage exit, watch in hand. Previn, baton on stand,

17

hands in hip pockets, said to the orchestra, 'There was some rhythmic carelessness, wasn't there? That's because it's just a rehearsal, right?' He was grinning. '*Somebody* nod.'

CHAPTER 2

Previn arrived at Heinz Hall early Thursday night for the eight-o'clock concert. He likes to relax a bit, talk to orchestra members, before going to his dressing room to change from jeans and shirt to white tie and tails. At eight sharp, he made his way down the long corridor and a dogleg left and walked about twenty paces to the stage entrance. The programme was a crowd pleaser, and a big success with the audience. The tricky string passage in the Rachmaninoff went so well that it was confident, even jubilant, and in the Brahms Gutiérrez was in great form. Previn has said of him, 'I've never seen such a soloist. He's so intense, gets into the music so much, if you asked him what *country* he's in he couldn't tell you.' At the last note, Previn faced the orchestra during the first burst of applause. When there is no soloist, Previn always signals to the orchestra to stand before he turns to acknowledge the applause. Now, in lieu of a handshake, he gave Gutiérrez a bear hug, and then signalled to the orchestra members to stand. He had removed his glasses, 'not for reasons of vanity,' he later told me. 'They're *steamed*, I can't see.' Pittsburgh audiences are sometimes said to be staid, but they called Gutiérrez and Previn back for a number of bows, and toward the end everyone in the audience was standing and applauding.

In the greenroom, Previn and Gutiérrez accepted congratulations from several dozen music lovers, and then Previn went to his room to change. He emerged wearing a dark suit, a pale-blue shirt and, instead of a tie, a paisley silk scarf around his neck. Gutiérrez's wife, Patricia, was standing next to her husband in the greenroom when Previn returned. A slender, brown-haired young woman, a pianist herself – she met Gutiérrez at Aspen, and they

19

both studied at Juilliard – she travels everywhere with her husband. He suffers from stage fright, and she said to Previn, 'He came out smiling tonight. I've never seen that before. What happened?'

Previn said, 'I told him a ribald joke – not for ladies' ears.'

On another night, another concert, Previn approached the stage door with Itzhak Perlman. The two were whistling the theme from 'The Andy Griffith Show' in thirds – at Perlman's challenge. When they reached the door, Previn said, 'Itz, if you weren't such a bundle of nerves you could be a big star.'

Most conductors in America today are more modest in demeanour than their predecessors were. Cloaks and entourages are out, and so is the long black limousine. Previn had invited the Gutiérrezes to dinner, and out on the street a car was waiting. The three got into the back seat of a pale blue four-door Oldsmobile and, with a cluster of hangers-on watching, were driven off into the night.

Monday is a 'dark' day at Heinz Hall – no rehearsals. On Tuesday, at ten, Previn began rehearsals for the coming weekend concerts. The programme this time was the Piston Symphony No. 6; the Mozart Violin Concerto No. 3, in G-Major, with Young-Uck Kim as the soloist; and the Beethoven Symphony No. 5. A local critic had complained that Previn never scheduled Beethoven, and implied that he was afraid to, but Previn says that William Steinberg conducted all but one of the symphonies in his last few seasons with the orchestra, so it seemed better to wait awhile. Previn came in from the street lugging a card table. He said, 'I look like a character in search of a Pinter play.' He had been composing sitting on the floor in his apartment, legs extended under a coffee table, so he could use the table's surface for large score paper. He was beginning to complain of backaches, and hoped that the new table would give him a more comfortable work space.

Previn began the morning's rehearsal with the Beethoven Fifth. Of the famous first four notes, he said, 'No accents. They are all absolutely even – hammered home every time.' He had indicated a slow tempo, to the disgruntlement of many of the musicians. He said, 'Now that you know it's slower than you expected, give it time.' He concentrated on trouble spots in the Piston, and told the orchestra, which would be giving a free pops concert on Wednesday night in the sixteen-thousand-seat Civic Arena, 'You can practice the Piston during the 1812 Overture.' For the Mozart, the orchestra was reduced to chamber-music size. Previn thinks that Young-Uck Kim plays better Mozart than any violinist he knows. Kim, a trim, slim, wiry young man, does a certain amount of bobbing and weaving while he plays, but his Mozart is truly stunning – lilting and light at times, phrased beautifully always.

After the rehearsal, Previn stayed to hear six finalists audition for the principal-second-violin chair. An audition is the most painful thing an orchestra musician can go through, since an entire career may ride on the outcome, and ordinarily the number of openings is far exceeded by the number of players. When the Pittsburgh Symphony has an opening, an ad is placed in the *International Musician*, a monthly magazine published by the American Federation of Musicians. A hundred and eight tuba players once applied for a single opening. At auditions, the aspirants will be asked to play snatches of standard orchestral repertoire chosen for their technical difficulties; to sight-read works, also difficult and usually modern (sometimes still in unpublished manuscript, to preclude a prior encounter with the work, for all too often a professional auditioner who has studied the tricky passages and been chosen can only flounder in an orchestra); and to play prepared selections from the instrument's solo repertoire. There is a shortage of string players now; high schools across America have abandoned orchestras and concentrated on bands, and only thirty-one violinists came to Pittsburgh for the audition – conservatory graduates and people from lesser orchestras who wanted to move up. Three Pittsburgh seconds also tried out. The Pittsburgh Symphony, which is backed by a rich community and has a strong union, is one of about a dozen orchestras in the United States that have a fifty-two-week contract. Equally important, the orchestra ranks high: sixth or seventh now, after the big five – Boston, Cleveland, Chicago, Philadelphia, and New York. The other sixth or seventh is the Los Angeles Philharmonic.

Feeling would run high at this audition. Of the six finalists, two were Pittsburgh players. Every orchestra has its caste system: all players are ranked, and within any section there's more honour in being in the front than in the back. Players in the rear of the sections sometimes feel they aren't heard or seen; there's always a certain amount of chair-shifting to find an unobstructed view of the conductor; and if there's deadwood in an orchestra both audiences and colleagues assume that the scarcely visible players are the culprits. In addition, in works that call for a reduced orchestra – Mozart, Haydn, early Beethoven symphonies, for instance – the back half of a section doesn't play at all. The rear of a string section can be a purgatory for the restless – a situation that is somewhat alleviated by a recent practice of some music directors (Previn is one) of rotating string players from the third stand through the last, and listing the players' names in the programme alphabetically rather than in cruel order of importance. There is honour and dignity in being seated at the first two stands – especially the principal seat – and usually more money, too.

In Heinz Hall to hear the auditions were members from all five string sections – including, of course, Siegal – who, as members of the audition committee, would choose the new principle second. Previn said to Siegal, 'I just *hate* these things. They do more harm than good. Sometimes they seem to tear the orchestra apart.' (Fortunately, there's not a lot of mobility in the Pittsburgh now. Only twenty-seven members have retired or moved to other orchestras and been replaced since Previn arrived, in 1976. During Fritz Reiner's reign – of terror – between 1937 and 1947, the attrition rate one year was forty-five per cent. One member of that forty-five per cent – a string bass – earned immortality during a concert by whipping out a long spyglass and training it on Reiner's minuscule beat. Though he was summarily fired, he's a hero, almost a folk figure, to orchestra members everywhere.)

In the finals, it was almost a toss-up between two Pittsburgh players – a young man, and an older woman with impressive orchestral credentials. The audition committee picked the young man, to the surprise of the woman, who was hurt and said to a friend, 'I could *phone* in my part from the back of that section.' Sometimes a younger player has yet to lose the conservatory bloom, the lovely soloist sound, and has more dazzling repertoire in his fingers than a longtime orchestra player. Previn thought both musicians were equally good, and after giving the matter some thought he exercised a music director's prerogative to overrule an orchestra-committee decision, and made the two violinists co-principals. In 1981, Previn prefaced a performance of the Beethoven Ninth Symphony with a Vivaldi concerto for four violins. He used as soloists three second violinists and one first, to show Pittsburgh audiences how good *all* his string players are, and to give the musicians a chance to be heard. The Vivaldi was such a success – impeccable technique and beautifully matched tone and phrasing, not to mention radiant pride – that Previn planned to do similar works in the future, so that everyone in the orchestra would have a chance to shine.

At the performance Friday night, the audience gave Previn and the orchestra a standing ovation after the Beethoven. Backstage, one of the slow-tempo dissidents admitted to me that he had been wrong – that the evening's Beethoven was a high point for him in many years of orchestra playing.

Among the audience members in the greenroom after the concert were Mr and Mrs Jerome Apt. Previn kissed Joan Apt on each cheek and, at arm's length, admired her blue fox jacket. After he had changed into street clothes – dark suit, no tie, scarf – he and Kim were driven by the Apts to their home for dinner. Jerome Apt is an engineer, and his wife makes a full-time career of supporting the arts. She is on more boards than she can name offhand, including the symphony's, and when Previn arrived in the city she invited him to dinner. He finds her gracious and generous and so respectful of his desire to avoid large groups that he has been back many times. The dinners are restricted to Previn and anyone he chooses to invite. At intermission, Mrs Apt, talking with friends and drinking champagne in the grand-tier lobby, says that she's just going to 'pop something in the oven', but dinner will be served by a maid and will consist of something like veal marsala, asparagus with hollandaise sauce, a crisp salad made of a variety of greens, and a very fine red wine. This evening would be filled with anecdotes. Kim and Previn are good friends (Previn calls Kim Korea's Warren Beatty because of his attraction to women), and Previn says that he and Kim – and everyone else he regularly engages for concerts, for that matter – pick up almost where they left off, in midsentence, a year or two before. They all have in common certain frames of reference – the mention of a name that will recall a wild incident and provoke explosions of laughter; something special that happened at a certain performance; a friend that one has seen more recently than the other; with Kim, in particular, things that happened in Korea: a family meal at which Previn ate a small carrot-size thing that was supposed to be lightly grated, as a hot spice. Previn tells the story on himself, and not just at the Apts's: 'I felt as if I'd put a grenade in my mouth and pulled the pin. I thought I would die. I didn't think it would be honourable to spit it out. They are such polite, *caring* people. They watched in amazement. I survived, obviously, but for *days* I drank gallons of water.'

Previn can be diffident, introverted, quiet and cool, impassive, reclusive, and rejecting – to the shock of new acquaintances and the dismay of old friends – but on television he is a different, consistent man: informative, even brilliant, and warm and gracious. As a matter of fact, he appears to be more relaxed in front of the cameras than he is in a friend's living-room. He was in his fourteenth year of broadcasting a variety of programmes for the BBC. These included the 'Omnibus' series, which was built around an idea and had prepared scripts. One such programme was 'Fidelio Finke, Where Are You?' Previn noticed ads for Finke's music on all the Breitkopf scores he bought. He'd never heard of the East German composer, so he looked up Finke's music and played some of it with the London Symphony Orchestra, and enjoyed speculating about composers who vanished without much of a trace, and why it happened to them. The other series, 'André Previn's Music Night', also featured the LSO, playing familiar classical music, offering it to people who in their entire lives would never have a chance to go to a concert. Previn discussed the music and talked about the composers extemporaneously – 'removed the upper-class, high-altar aspects from classical music', according to one friend. And the late Ian Englemann, who directed a great many of the programmes until his death, in 1981, once said, 'In England, André Previn *is* music.'

In 1976, there were people in America who had never heard of Previn and some who had forgotten about him. And in that year 'Pittsburgh' evoked the Pirates and the Steelers and just plain steel. In January of that year, John Goberman, the innovator and producer of the 'Live from Lincoln Center' programmes, chose Previn conducting the New York Philharmonic for the first broadcast. Goberman was familiar with Previn's BBC work, and the programme included an intermission talk between Previn and the orchestra's president, Carlos Moseley. The following year,

Previn began his own series, 'Previn and the Pittsburgh', which consisted of eight taped broadcasts and was misnamed, since not all the programmes featured the Pittsburgh. The orchestra concerts, which were preceded by Previn's talking about the music the audience was to hear, included works by Mozart, with Previn playing the Piano Concerto No. 20 in D-Minor; Tchaikovsky and Stravinsky, with Gutiérrez as the soloist in the Tchaikovsky Concerto; Debussy and Ravel, with Thomas Hoving and Previn discussing – arguing about, actually – the Impressionist movement in art and its influence on music; and an entire hour of Richard Strauss's 'Alpine' Symphony, which Previn, off camera, affectionately called 'a piece of strudel'. Itzhak Perlman played the Sibelius Violin Concerto and 'Two Little Serenades', composed by Previn for Perlman for the occasion of the birth of the Perlmans' first child. Since Previn didn't know if the baby would be a boy or a girl, and didn't want to write something 'yellow', one piece is masculine and one is feminine, and when Noah was born Previn gave both pieces to the Perlmans and said, 'Now you owe me another baby.' Previn paid homage to the jazz world by inviting Oscar Peterson and Ella Fitzgerald for separate programmes. Previn introduced Miss Fitzgerald by saying, 'Orchestras tune to an A given by the oboe, because it is the purest sound. They could just as easily tune to an A given by Ella.' He added, 'Musicians enjoy naming whom they consider the best on different instruments – ranking them. Mention jazz singers, and the choice is unanimous – Ella.' Previn can be scathing about Hollywood ('If I think about it, I can miss it for upward of two minutes'), yet he devoted two programmes to film music. Adolph Green once said that Previn used cue cards more gracefully than anyone else he'd seen on television, but when he and Betty Comden came to Pittsburgh to be on a programme honouring them he discovered that Previn rarely used cue cards – or notes, or anything. He just talked, and proved the truth of what another friend, the playwright Tom Stoppard, said – that

Previn automatically speaks in perfect syntax. There were several chamber-music programmes with Isaac Stern, Pinchas Zukerman, Nathaniel Rosen, and Yehudi Menuhin. Rosen also appeared as the cello soloist in Strauss's 'Don Quixote'. A string on his cello broke during the concert, and the orchestra stayed on to retape the piece. Another string broke, and Previn remained calm while Rosen was changing them. No one had ever seen Previn lose his temper in front of an orchestra, but then the producer of the series, Stephen Dick, had to tell him, under the heat of the television lights, that a camera – the one trained on Rosen – was not working. Previn erupted into a parody of rage, and said, 'Well, buy a *new* one!' Sixty thousand dollars. He later apologised to Dick, and said he'd exploded on behalf of the orchestra – kept overtime, and undoubtedly hot and tired and frustrated. There was a ninety-minute special devoted to the Brahms *Requiem*. It is one of Previn's favourite pieces, and, though he is accustomed to shifting gears, preparing the next programme ('I *can't* have a long affair with a certain piece; it's part of my profession to move on'), whenever he does the *Requiem* he consults his calendar to see when he will next have a chance to do it: London in 1982, Vienna in 1983. He is reassured.

In 1979, the money ran out, and there were no more programmes. While I was in Pittsburgh, I went to WQED to talk to Stephen Dick. A man of medium height, with a brown beard and greyish-brown glasses, Dick has a casual, nonchalant manner that disguises a keen intelligence, and on the subject of Previn he was almost bursting with admiration. He said, 'That guy is amazing. I'm a writer, for God's sake. I tell André I need two more minutes on, say, Beethoven. He'll light a cigarette, pace up and down once, and out comes a hundred and twenty *seconds* about Beethoven – clear and lucid and perfect. You can imagine how that makes me feel.' He shrugged, and laughed at himself. 'We put information on five-by-eight cards for André, and he'll glance at them and throw them away.' Previn is not impressed by his own television expertise. He says, 'I've been in and out of recording studios since I was a kid. I'm used to it.'

Dick showed me a promotion tape he'd put together to attract sponsors for the programmes. It begins with snatches of Carl Orff; continues with Previn telling Isaac Stern an amusing anecdote about floundering around in the Paris Conservatory when he was nine; Previn playing Scott Joplin with Itzhak Perlman; a voice-over listing all of Previn's talents; and, at the end, a few minutes of the Brahms *Requiem*. The camera is on the orchestra, and then it zooms in on Previn. On his face is a look of tenderness and love and joy. Dick said, 'He's not doing that for the camera.'

CHAPTER 3

One sunny afternoon, I went to see Previn in his apartment high up on Mount Washington, a section of Pittsburgh known for its expensive restaurants and scenic views. Previn enjoys the unusual. He and Tom Stoppard exchange newspaper clippings about the bizarre but true: pigs escape from a pen in the English countryside and eat a private plane on the next estate. It pleases Previn that when the architect of his building was not permitted to build the high rise up, he built it down, instead, and to get to Previn's apartment from the lobby you take a lift down to the ninth floor. I had buzzed his apartment on the intercom, and he was standing at the end of the hall, his door open. The hall was uncarpeted, the walls grey, with no windows or pictures, and he said, 'Doesn't it look just like a women's prison?'

Immediately inside the door is a foyer, and to the left is a sizable modern kitchen, with a counter that opens into the living room, directly ahead. The far wall of the living room is floor-to-ceiling sliding glass doors, open on this sunny day. There is a small terrace, and a view of all of Pittsburgh from this apartment hanging on a mountainside. Clearly visible are the Hilton Hotel; Point State Park, with its towering fountain (the first thing that football fans see when they watch a televised Pittsburgh Steelers game); Three Rivers Stadium; and the confluence of the three rivers – the Ohio, the Allegheny, and the Monongahela. Inside, the walls and wall-to-wall carpeting are off-white, and the furnishings include a long beige suède sofa, with a coffee table in front; a black leather Eames chair, with matching footstool; and, filling the corner, a concert-grand Baldwin. The foyer wall holds stereo equipment and records. There are some touches of colour in the room on

29

the piano, a three-foot-high Accorsi tree of letters – all the letters of the alphabet carved from wood and painted different bright colours – and on the walls several modern paintings, mostly in blues and greens, 'an overflow from my Surrey collection'.

In Previn's publicity pictures – glossies that Columbia Artists Management has been sending out for years – a wedding band is visible on his left hand. The ring was gone; he and his third wife, Mia Farrow, were divorced. On the piano were framed pictures of their children: non-identical twins, Sascha and Matthew, ten; Fletcher, six; and three little girls whom Previn and Miss Farrow adopted – Daisy, Lark, and Soon-Yi, aged five, six, and seven respectively. (Previn was conducting a concert in Korea in the early seventies, and he went to an orphanage with a musician intent on adopting a baby. Previn was so moved at the sight of hundreds of little babies, in cardboard boxes, covered with newspapers, that, if it weren't for the red tape, he said, 'I would have on the spot taken as many as I could carry out'. Back in Surrey, he discussed it with Miss Farrow, and they subsequently adopted the three children.) Lark and Daisy are Vietnamese; Soon-Yi is Korean. There are two daughters, now adults, from his marriage to Betty Bennett, a jazz singer. There were no children from his marriage to the lyricist Dory Langdon, but there was an immense art collection, which went to her as part of the divorce agreement. Previn is pleased that a woman who loves the collection got it, rather than one who might have sold it for furs and diamonds. He thinks that a fondness for furs and diamonds is an indication of a character flaw, and, that opinion aside, he does not talk about his personal life. Further, he deplores people in the public eye who do – people who use their access to the press to air private grievances.

Previn said, 'The twins live with me, in Surrey, and the others are with their mother, in New York.' Previn's friends speak of him as a devoted father, patriarchal in a way – the children, at his request, call him Papa – but

30

loving and wonderful with them. Previn said, 'When the twins were young – before it was time for school – I often took them with me, wherever I was conducting. I see the others whenever I'm in New York, and we all get together summers and holidays. Fletcher has learned the long-distance dialling system, and he calls me night and day. That pleases me very much.' He lingered at the piano, looking at the pictures. He said, 'The separations are killing. The twins love their nanny and their school, and when I go away they know I'll be back. But it tears me apart, in about fourteen directions.' Matthew and Daisy have shown an interest in music. Matthew is taking piano and violin lessons, and to save him from the boredom of a beginner's repertoire Previn composed and had published ten piano pieces for the advanced beginner. On the cover is a photograph of Previn and Matthew, and the title is 'Matthew's Piano Book'. Previn's apartment has two large bedrooms and two baths – plenty of room for the twins when they come to visit. Previn said, 'Once when they came to see me, I took them to the Apts' for dinner. Matthew shook hands with Joan Apt and said, "It's nice to meet you, Mrs Apartment." Isn't that lovely?'

I sat on the sofa, and Previn sank into the Eames chair. I asked him how many concerts he did in a year, and he said, 'I do fewer than a hundred now – not counting recordings. I think this season I will have done ninety-three. I'm not sure of that figure. You see, I have the luxury of' – he searched for the right word – 'permanence. I know all the people in this orchestra. I have friends in town, a place to store my stuff, to live when I'm here. Every year, I know that for four months I'm in Pittsburgh. Now, *soloists*. They travel sometimes forty-four weeks out of a year. They're never in any city more than a week at a time. I would find that killing. There are many evenings, though, when I come home and start talking to the furniture. I'm *offered* invitations, but usually I can't accept. I spend my evenings studying, working, preparing, and the times I have a casual evening off are very few. You

31

know, sometimes I'm very cynical about my profession, but no matter how grim it gets you *do* get the reward of the music. You get it many days every week, and then it becomes worthwhile. I'm just stuck with that attitude. A career in music, when you get to a certain point, a certain success – it takes all your effort just to *stay* there. I don't deny that it's pleasant to make the fees that I make now, and it pleases me that I've got to the point where doing what I really adore doing pays me much more than I could ever have made in Hollywood. That's good to know. But the real point, the way I feel, is that I'm just *crazy* about music, and if a day goes by in which I don't have some involvement with it – be it practising, studying a score, composing – it's a day lost forever, and I'm bereft. When I get tired of studying a score, and the silence gets to me, it's a real pleasure to go to the piano and really work on, say, the Ravel Trio – straighten out all the snarls.'

An article in the *New York Times* about conductors in America mentioned the importance of a conductor as a social being. It helps if he's attractive, and the happiest ones have wives to help out. And parties are a must. The women who had come to the open rehearsal were contributors. Previn said, 'I admire what they do. They're essential to the orchestra, and I try to help out, coöperate, whenever I can. But I don't like to go to big "functions", as they call them. It's not disdain on my part. When I walk into a room and there are more than a hundred people, all standing and talking, with drinks in hand, I genuinely panic, and I wind up in a corner – literally and figuratively – with my back against the wall, sweating like crazy, and wishing I were dead. After about forty-five minutes, I have to excuse myself and go into a bathroom. I splash cold water on my face, and sit on a cold tile floor, if possible, until I get my bearings. I go back once more into the breach – *Henry V?* – and it takes more out of me than the complete Mahler cycle. I really, genuinely suffer. It's so complex. People come up out of kindness, a desire to flatter – admirable things to be on the receiving end of. It's

32

a physical thing. I feel that the walls are closing in. I really hate it. During the time I'm talking to people, I think I do it rather well, but there's that sudden moment of panic when I feel that if I don't get some air, some space around me, I'm going to fall down. It's given me a reputation here for being violently anti-social. Some people feel that a reception, a fund-raiser, is successful only if a hundred people come. And I just go to pieces. I like people. I just can't handle them in large numbers. I don't react well to what I call "relentless hospitality". If I go with a friend, or perhaps a soloist, it's half the terror. But it would have to be a very close friend, to inflict that on. I seem to have thousands of acquaintances but very few close friends.' He defined a close friend as someone whom he could call at three in the morning and say, 'Meet me at the airport. No questions asked.'

Previn offered me some coffee – instant – and went into the kitchen to heat the water. He has said that if he changes a light bulb all of Surrey blacks out and he approached the stove warily. (He once complained to Kaplan that he liked vanilla yogurt, but couldn't find it in Pittsburgh. Kaplan suggested that he buy plain yogurt and just add a drop of vanilla. Previn said, 'Oh, Kap, you know I don't want to get into cooking.') While the water was heating, Previn talked. 'This period has been un-believable. There have been more problems upstairs than you can imagine. Administration, auditions, tour replace-ments, schedules. Every day, some major or minor disaster occurs, and they all take so many discussions. So many people involved, and everybody talks and talks and talks. So much time that I would have enjoyed spending on studying, or practising, or writing. And nothing's been solved. We're whittling away at it.'

I had been to the trio concert, and I complimented him on the performance. I remarked that it was odd, though, that the group didn't have a name.

Previn said, 'I don't want to use my name, and since management takes a dim view of us, I don't want to use

33

"Pittsburgh". I don't know why they look askance at us. Lots of people in the orchestra play outside jobs – chamber music. Management seems to feel that it diminishes my status with the orchestra, and I don't understand that. A few years ago, Annie and Herb and I just had some fun, and then when we decided to play a couple of concerts at the Y there was some hell raised. I said that if I were to conduct some other orchestra in Pittsburgh they would have a point, but I just like to play the piano, and I want that privilege. Chamber music is the ultimate thrill in music for a conductor. I went to management and, not as a challenge, said, 'I don't care *who* presents these concerts, nor do Annie and Herb. Pay us what the Y pays us and we'll give the concerts in Heinz, if you like, or wherever you like.' They asked me what the Y paid, and turned green when I told them. I've never missed a rehearsal, been unavailable when I should be doing something. They gave up, but it's been made clear to me that they view the whole endeavour like a parent watching a child walk a tightrope across the Grand Canyon. None of it makes sense. I've played chamber music all my life – in Hollywood and during the jazz years. Three years in a row, I played the complete Beethoven trios with members of the Roth Quartet, and I recorded two quartets with them. It's an essential part of my life. When I conduct in Vienna, I *always* play chamber music with people from the Vienna Philharmonic. I even make records with them. And I play in public with the quartet from the Chicago Symphony. There are very few times when I just dig my heels in, but this time I did.'

The kettle in the kitchen whistled, and Previn went in to make the coffee. He returned with two cups, put them on the coffee table, and stretched out on the rug, elbow on floor, head propped on hand, and talked.

Previn was born in Berlin in April of 1929, the second son and third and last child in the family. His parents were

Jack and Charlotte Prewin – as the name was spelled in Germany. Jack Prewin was a successful lawyer, and was also an excellent amateur pianist and an almost feverish music lover. All three children were given piano lessons, but only André liked them from the start, and showed signs of genius. When he was six, he was enrolled in the Berlin conservatory, or Hochschule für Musik. His father took him to many concerts – some of them rather heavy going for a child. On one occasion, it was Richard Strauss's one-act opera, *Salome*, and, after an intermission, the ballet 'Coppélia'. Previn likes to tell friends that for many years he thought John the Baptist was beheaded in a toy shop.

In 1938, Previn's father was told that André was no longer welcome at the conservatory – even though he'd been given a full scholarship in recognition of his promise – because he was Jewish. Jack Prewin, who had already applied for American visas and was waiting for their numbers to come up, took the family to Paris immediately, ostensibly for the weekend. Once, Previn appeared on the 'Dick Cavett Show', and he described the family's departure to Cavett. Previn said, 'We took just one bag, and left everything we owned behind. I didn't understand why we were leaving, and was too young to be traumatised by the experience. For me, it was "Oh, boy! Everybody off to the plane!" My parents handled it very well. It wasn't until years later that I understood what they'd been through.' (He told a friend another thing he remembers from his Berlin childhood: a sign on a park bench that said 'No Dogs, No Bicycles, No Jews.' He added wryly, 'At least they got the order right.')

It took nine months for the visas to arrive, and while the family was in Paris Previn's father enrolled André in the Paris conservatory. Previn said, 'I remember the conservatory mostly because of a wonderful, wild theory professor I had. He taught not just theory but the beginnings of knowledge of instruments. He wore flowing robes, and on his way down the hall to the classroom he would stop one of us and say, "*Quick*! What's the lowest note on the oboe?" We would say, "I beg your pardon, I didn't hear you", and he would say, "Too late, too late!" We were terrified. We hid in lockers to avoid his questions, but we looked the answers up later, and we *never* forgot them.' He added, 'Sometimes people ask me if I resented not having a normal childhood. *I* didn't know it wasn't normal. I thought everyone practised eight hours a day.'

By what was almost a quirk of fate, the Previns went to Los Angeles instead of New York when they arrived in the United States. Previn's father had a cousin, Brooklyn-born, whom everyone in the family called Uncle Charlie. He was a musician who had moved to the Coast and gone to work at Universal Studios as a conductor. He and Jascha Heifetz, who was a friend of Previn's mother's, both vouched for the family. For reasons of language and California state law, Previn's father was not allowed to practise law, so he started giving piano lessons. Previn said, 'In terms of being a piano teacher, the accent was an advantage.' Previn learned English, with the help of a dictionary, by 'reading things like comic books, anything I could pick up', he told me, 'and sitting through the same movies countless times'. He added, 'I was more or less stuffed into public school, and, not realising how difficult that was, I somehow managed.' Previn's father found theory and composition teachers and, with Heifetz's help, a piano teacher for his son, and since the family was 'dirt poor', Previn said, once he was acclimatised he began getting work at local radio stations – writing arrangements and sometimes playing, doing anything to help out. One of his after-school jobs was playing the piano for silent films in a little theatre in Hollywood, on North Highland Avenue. Previn said, 'In every city, there always seems to be an audience for those films – I don't know why. I never got to pre-see the movies, and as long as they were fairly innocuous there were no problems. But one film was ambitious in so far as it kept vacillating between Biblical times and the twenties, when it was made. It may have been *Intolerance*, directed by D.W. Griffith. It kept switching back and forth from the Sermon on the Mount and the flappers. The flappers seemed to me to go on forever, doing some kind of supposedly debauched dance. And I got myself heavily into Charlestons and didn't look up. When I *did* look up, I was playing "Twelfth Street Rag" to the Crucifixion, which got me fired *very* rapidly. Since I was making six dollars a day, it didn't hurt too badly.' He had fantasies of becoming a conductor, but he realised that child conductors were anathema. Previn had all the ingredients for becoming a pianist of blinding virtuosity, but he seems never to have even considered being a concert pianist. Today, innumerable concert artists are taking up conducting, to expand their repertoire and to avoid being limited to the same concertos, and perhaps Previn was blessed with foresight. He's also had the best of both worlds. In his role as conductor, he regularly plays piano concertos and conducts from the keyboard. He has recorded a number of concertos, and has also recorded two albums of Rachmaninoff two-piano works with Vladimir Ashkenazy. In New York, in 1980, Gutiérrez was the soloist in the Prokofieff Third Piano Concerto, and the *New York Times* critic Harold Schonberg praised Previn as a conductor and added, 'Mr Previn. . .himself is a good enough pianist to handle the Prokofieff Third.' Of that, Previn says, 'Nonsense. I was never that kind of pianist.'

Previn described his entry into Hollywood as 'surreal'. He had watched his uncle conduct many times at Universal Studios, but the two had agreed that they wouldn't use one another in the film world ('I have this nephew who. . .' 'I have this uncle who. . .'). Previn calls his Hollywood period his 'Esther Williams days'. Previn said, 'At that time, the late forties, movies were made the way television programmes are today – ground out, one after another. José Iturbi was making a film with Jane Powell. In one scene, he played a piano covered with mirrors. He was supposed to play some kind of jazz, and he couldn't.' When Previn was fourteen, he stumbled on an Art Tatum recording of 'Sweet Lorraine', and he was stunned by what he heard. He'd always thought that jazz was 'men in funny hats playing in a hotel band'. He listened to the Tatum record repeatedly, and copied what Tatum played 'note for bloody note'. Previn developed a jazz style that he calls 'highly derivative', but that was sufficient for the purpose of his playing on numerous radio broadcasts. Someone at MGM who had heard several of the broadcasts suggested that Previn be hired to write some jazz for Iturbi. 'I'm sure it occurred to them that because I was sixteen I wouldn't charge them a lot,' Previn said to me. 'So I did it, and after I handed it in I heard that they were going to give it to an orchestrator for an orchestral background. This being Hollywood, just plain piano wouldn't be enough. I asked to do the orchestration, and they used what I did, and I had a wonderful time. They wanted me to finish school there – I had a semester to go – but I wasn't that enamoured of graduating with Butch Jenkins, an awful little kid in pictures then.'

Although it has been a long time since Previn was in Hollywood, he remains vivid to the people he worked with and became friends with. Billy Wilder, who directed *Irma La Douce* – a film that brought Previn one of four Academy Awards – is a good friend of his to this day. Wilder counts Previn among a handful of the most interesting, entertaining people he knows. He says, 'There's never a dull second with André, and we seem to talk about everything but music.' An avid art collector, Wilder guided Previn through galleries and museums. He likes to speculate about what kind of career Previn would have had if he'd come out of the Leningrad conservatory, say, instead of Hollywood, and observes, 'After all, even Thomas Mann was demeaned by his years in California.' Adolph Green says Previn was 'still a baby – barely in his teens' when they first met. 'There were lots of great musicians out there but very few extraordinary ones,' Green recalls. 'He was a hot potato. Everyone wanted to sponsor him; they all knew sooner or later he'd sweep over them. And no one knew where his future lay, because he was so multi-talented. He has a casual way of just making things happen – he's doing so *many* things all the time. He worked with various musical groups. One, in particular, he did a lot of recordings with – forgotten chamber works, or pieces not yet recorded. Once, they were rehearsing a Shostakovich piano trio, and there was something in the score that was ambiguous – they didn't know what Shostakovich was getting at musically. So André impulsively put in a call to the Soviet Union, and he got Shostakovich, and they went over the score together. And this was years before André ever conducted anything. He reasoned, "What the hell, Shostakovich isn't dead; let's give it a whirl." There are no obstacles for André.'

While Previn was finishing high school and working at MGM, he was also trying to write flawless fugues and string quartets. He studied with the composer Joseph Achron – also a famous pedagogue who delighted in finding mistakes. Previn said, 'He was very tough, and he *hated* it if you did something well. He told me to compose a four-part fugue for string quartet, and I worked on it until I was blue in the face. Achron read through it several times, and said, "I can't believe that you haven't made a mistake. Give me another few minutes." He read through it again, and suddenly he said, "Ah-ha!" He pointed to the page and said, "Hidden octaves!" He took a blue grease pencil, slashed his way through all the pages, threw them on the floor, and said, "Go home and do it again." At that point – I know there's fratricide and infanticide. I don't know what teacher-icide is, but I seriously considered it.' Previn's odd environment, as it turned out, provided him with a music education that a Juilliard student could envy. The principal cellist of the MGM studio orchestra, Willem Vandenberg, was a close friend of the violinist Joseph Szigeti, who was in California on a sabbatical. Szigeti championed new music, and was inundated with scores from all over the world – usually violin-and-piano sonatas. He was temporarily without an accompanist, and Vandenberg told Szigeti about Previn – told him that Previn could sight-read anything. (Previn said, 'My father was dead set on my being a good musician, as opposed to a good mechanical pianist. Every night of my life, he would bring out new music, put it in front of me, and say, "Play it. Play it at tempo. Damn the mistakes." I learned to cheat, learned what to leave out while still getting the feel of the music.' Previn's father also force-fed Bach fugues into Previn so diligently and relentlessly that Previn came to hate Bach – a feeling he has outgrown.) Vandenberg drove Previn to Szigeti's house, and, according to Previn, he and Szigeti 'ploughed through Bulgarian sonatas', and Previn was invited to come back the following week. At the next session, Szigeti suggested that Vandenberg get his cello out of his car, and that, for a change of pace, the three play some trios. He said they would begin with Previn's favourite Beethoven, whatever it might be. Previn told me, 'With the rudeness of innocence, I said, "I don't have a favourite. I don't know any of them." Szigeti was truly shocked that I'd never played *any* of the standard trios – Beethoven, Brahms, Schubert.' From that night on, every Monday for over twenty weeks the three met to play trios. Since Previn didn't know which ones they would be playing, he couldn't have practised them even if he had had the time. Previn said, 'Unless *technically* a thing fell apart, we would play through a big movement without stops, and then Szigeti would go back and point out things that could have been done, and things we'd done that he didn't like. He would talk about the whole piece – not just technical improvements – and what else Beethoven, say, wrote in that period, and how it related to other things he composed. He never did it professorially. It was *so* generous of him – so magnanimous. He could have picked up the phone and got any number of great pianists to play trios with him. I saw his daughter in London not long ago, and told her. It pleased her.'

While Previn was talking, the telephone rang. When he answers the phone his voice is flat, disembodied – the voice of a man who has just shut all the windows and turned on the gas. When he recognizes the caller as a friend – in this case it was Itzhak Perlman, inquiring about the jazz-recording session – he goes not into gear but into overdrive. 'Bubbie! Don't worry! You can sight-read it. No. . . Even if you had it, you'd read it through and say, "What's all the screaming about?" It's all connected with the rest of the group, and when you come here you and I will sit down and play through it a couple of evenings, and we'll laugh a lot. . . Well, what I've done is written out what I politely call suggested choruses, and you play those if you can't think of nothing. And if you can, you can play anything you want. There's nothing to it. They're all laid out, so that the order of events – who plays what, where, and when – is totally down on paper. . . Well, if it were a true jazz session you'd kind of improvise, but in this case, because we won't have those all-night sessions, I've written out a real road map on every tune, so that there's no question. If you suddenly discover you can improvise, we'll back you. These things are extremely flexible. Bring some Gershwin, Rodgers and Hart, Cole Porter, and we'll take it from there, because the guys will know all that stuff. It will be terrific. I think we'll get hysterical with laughter. . . Listen, I'm worried about the Korngold. You're worried about the blues. . . Wednesday morning, I'll work on "Appalachian Spring", Wednesday afternoon, the tuttis of Korngold and Conus, and by Thursday morning, eleven, I'll be some ready for you. . . Listen, baby, you wanted to record this stuff. You wanted the Tedesco, for Christ's sake. I'm saving you from yourself, Itzhak. . . I know, it's very pretty. It's like Exodus. Jesus. . .I know Heifetz's Korngold record, and I looked at the score. Even the great man cheats in that last movement. . . Well, if it's impossible for you it's impossible for anybody. . . We'll record the blues next week. . . Some are a little complicated rhythmically, and I've

41

written some plain old pretty things. . . The thing I
adore is that you can't make no intercuts. . . Because it's
going to be different every *time*. You choose the best one,
and that's the end of it.' He laughed. 'I've been waiting for
this for ten years. . . OK, I ain't worried. Tell them to pick
you up in a rocket. . . OK. So long.' Previn was grinning
when he hung up. Returning to his place on the rug, he
stretched out again and said, 'There have always been
rumours that I was the head of the MGM music department. That's not true. I was just one of six or seven on the
staff.' Although he started at MGM composing and
orchestrating a piece, his work there was not, at first,
totally creative. He learned the craft of orchestrating
gradually, and spent many tedious hours as a rehearsal
pianist. 'John Williams and I were both rehearsal pianists,'
he said, 'and we've been good friends ever since.'

Williams says of this, 'No, no. André was well established as a film composer when we met. He encouraged
me to compose, introduced me to Hollywood producers,
was interested in every little tune I turned out. In the mid-
fifties, we did two LPs for RCA – "André Previn in
Hollywood" and "Soundstage". I did the orchestration
and conducted, and he was the piano soloist. Just his
asking me to do them was a wonderful help to me. He's
innately generous. He was always interested in other
people's work. And he was always a celebrity, at a time
when people weren't all that aware of what music meant
to a picture. He entertained a lot, and invitations to his
small dinner parties were prized. We have a mutual
friend, Alexander Courage, a film-music composer. Sandy
met André before I did, shortly after André arrived in
Hollywood. Sandy is a very literate, informed man, and
he claims that by the time André was eighteen he had read
more than all of us put together.'

Previn was assigned his first original score in 1948. 'It
was produced by a man called Robert Sisk, who used to be
with the Theatre Guild in New York. He was the one who
got me interested in first editions of books. He became a

producer, and for a man of his intellect he made very undistinguished pictures. They were terrible, but he was the first to ask me to write an entire score. The film was *The Sun Comes Up*, starring Jeanette MacDonald and Lassie. There was *lots* of music – wall-to-wall – because there was a lot of barking and hardly anybody spoke. Any Lassie movie has endless music, and I quite enjoyed that.' His second film score was for a film called *Scene of the Crime* – a detective story that involved the New York Police Department. Previn said, 'It all took place either in Brooklyn or the Bronx, and I ran it and decided there wasn't going to be much music in it. The producer told me he wanted, as a theme song, a Mexican tune called "Celita Linda". I went back to the cubbyhole I had as an office, and I thought, "*Why* does he want a Mexican song?". I thought maybe there was some subtlety in the film that I had missed, and I ran it again. I worried about it for three days, and then I went to the producer and said, "I'm sorry. Maybe you've got the wrong composer. What is the point of having 'Celita Linda' as the theme song?" The producer said, "It's my favourite".' He paused, and added, 'What can you do? Laugh? Swallow a scream? Dine out on a story like that? In those days, they had themselves driven to the commissary in a limousine. Twenty seconds. They thought it would last forever.'

Otherwise, for the most part, Previn was orchestrating other composers' works, and, in retrospect, some things that happened then seem funny, but some still outrage him. One producer, in particular, made especially successful musicals, with people like Mario Lanza and Kathryn Grayson. Previn said that the producer was extremely good at knowing what people in those days wanted to see, but was innocent about the arts. Previn was asked to provide a chamber-music scene in a movie starring Jane Powell. The producer wanted the scene to take place in Carnegie Hall and to include a piano. Previn picked the Schumann Piano Quintet, because he liked it and the studio would not have to pay a copyright fee. He used the principal strings from the MGM studio orchestra, and the five men recorded the first movement. The producer liked what he heard. He liked it so much that he called Previn and said it was a waste to do it with just five people. He wanted an orchestra, too. Previn said, 'I remember looking into the phone, as if I could see him, and I said, "But the word 'quintet' has an inherent meaning that you can't change." That went into a brick wall. He said, "It sounds crappy with those four guys, and I want you to do it with a great big orchestra." ' Previn refused, and was suspended, which meant he couldn't work for anyone else until what had turned into a war had been resolved. Previn said, 'The storm went on and on and on, and in the final product that scene does not exist. She never did go to that damned concert. Had the man *known* how dreadful an idea it was, and been cynical about it, that would have been unforgivable. But he didn't have the faintest idea. He thought, "It's a pretty tune, this is MGM, and why not have a big orchestra?" His innocence makes the story no less horrible but much more forgivable from a philosophical point of view.' (Previn's favourite Hollywood story happened before he got there. He said, 'Irving Thalberg – the *wunderkind* of the thirties – was very smart about movies but didn't know anything about music. He ran a picture once – so the story goes – and there was something in the score that he disliked. He said to one of his sycophants, "What is that in the music that I dislike so much?" And the man, who didn't know anything, either, said, "Oh, Mr Thalberg, that's a minor chord." He could also have said a major chord. He could have said a French horn. He could have said *anything*. He just wanted to get off the hook. Thalberg then dictated an interoffice memo, which was framed and hung in the MGM music library, and it was still there when I arrived. It said, "From the above date onward, there will be no minor chords in MGM music scores." It's *endearingly* horrifying, because he *meant* it. It was a sign I tried to steal, but I couldn't get it unscrewed from the wall.')

44

There's an apocryphal story that Previn's hands were filmed in place of Barbara Stanwyck's in a movie in which she played a concert pianist. Previn said, 'No, no. The director had photographed her, sitting at a piano, weaving around like a limbo dancer. Nobody could figure out what in hell she would be *playing* with that kind of body movement. You couldn't see her hands clearly. Miklós Rózsa did the score. I wrote something that would sound as if it were coming from somebody who was going through that kind of agony at the piano.'

Previn talked about MGM's Herbert Stothart, who, he said, did 'all the great pictures, and had done so since the advent of time'. Previn said, 'He was a charming man, phenomenal-looking, with an enormous mane of white hair and an imposing presence. He conducted like a demonic windmill, and got some very pleasant perform-ances out of the orchestra. Mr Stothart had a string of orchestrators, arrangers, ghostwriters, and other helpers, and was not above just writing out a melody line of eight bars and saying, "Here – write ten minutes of whatever." '

Previn was eighteen or so when he worked for Stothart, and one day Stothart gave Previn a melody line – 'an attractive theme, I must say' – and told Previn that it would be the title music, and wanted it 'huge, gigantic', adding, 'I don't care *how* many people you use in the orchestra. You can have a chorus, organ – *anything*.' Previn went home with the tune and proceeded to write what he called 'a lexicon of excesses'. It sounded to him like the end of 'The Pines of Rome'. When it came time to record the music, Stothart sat on a stool on the podium, with a lead sheet – the theme in treble clef, and the timings – in front of him. Previn sat on the first of three steps that led to the podium, so that if there were any questions from the players about their notes he could answer them. Previn said, 'Mr Stothart gave the downbeat, and this dreadful music came *roaring* out, like some enormous surf of bad taste, and at about the ninth climactic moment within the first three minutes, without slackening his beat, he leaned over to me and, in a tone of total surprise, said, "Did I write this?" '

Previn said that there were some really talented and dedicated people in Hollywood, and that it's a shame that all the memorable stories are about the quasi-charlatans. Another man he worked for, George Stoll, also didn't write. He had a lot of helpers, and a knack for getting the right people to help him. Previn said, 'He was the only man I've ever met who played the piano with his thumb. Most people who can't play use their index finger. I kind of admired that – just his thumb.' With his thumb, Stoll played Previn a theme that he wanted written for a big orchestra. Part of the theme was an octave above high C, and he told Previn that he wanted the trumpets on that. 'I told him not in that register, surely,' Previn said. 'He was on his way to a meeting – he was terrific at meetings, he conned *every*body – and he was in a hurry, and he said, "Of *course* in that register." I was desperate – again, I was just a kid. I said, "But, George, in that register – trumpets can't *play* up there." As he flew out the door, he shouted back, "Well, *try*!" I was completely stumped. What does that mean? Try. Who's trying? I wrote the trumpet parts in the normal register and put some piccolos above them, and it worked. He didn't notice.'

Previn had another story about George Stoll – he called it a wicked one, because, he said, Stoll was basically a nice man. Previn and an experienced orchestrator and composer, a Frenchman named Leo Arnaud, collaborated once on a project for Stoll. Stoll conducted, and dealt with the stars and the producers, and he felt that writing was the smallest part of being a composer. He threw an assignment at Previn and Arnaud that had to be done overnight. Previn said, '*Endless* music. It must have been eighty pages of score. I went to Leo's house, and we worked in tandem. Copyists came every two hours to stay ahead of it. Before we started, Leo, who had been in the business a long time, said, "You know, the copyists will barely have time to do the orchestra parts, and we'll have *no* time to make George one of his treble-clef lead sheets, so he's going to be stuck conducting from the score. As long as we're going to be up all night anyway, let's write every conceivable transposition possible." It was *so* childish of us. We wrote flutes in G, clarinets in A, horns in F, trumpets always in B-flat. We wrote cellos and trombones in tenor clef. There wasn't *anything* – except the fiddle line – that read the way it sounded. We staggered in in the morning, having literally been up all night writing, and handed George the score. He got up there on the rostrum, and of *course* there were questions.' At this point, Previn was up, pacing and gesticulating. 'George had *no* idea what he was looking at. And Leo and I, knowing this was coming, went into the control booth and, like six-year-olds, hid on the floor behind the control console. The first time someone said "What's my note?" George looked at the score and realised, "Christ, it's all transposed." He turned around and looked for us, but we were out of sight. And there was the most *frantic* uproar out there, with George *screaming* at the players, "With the money you guys make, *you* ought to know what your note is!" And one guy said, "What are you talking about? I just want to check whether it's a B-flat or not." This went on for a sweaty five minutes – a huge crescendo – and finally the producer, who was also in the booth, said, "If you guys don't come out of hiding and help him, you're both fired." ' Previn laughed. 'Those were the really infantile ways in which we had fun, and got even.'

Previn went to the kitchen to make more coffee, and when he came back he shut the sliding glass doors. The sun was setting – reflecting from the Hilton windows, and causing the three rivers to glisten – and the air was chilly.

Previn worked full time at MGM until 1950, when he was drafted, and he had the good fortune to be sent to San Francisco. He was stationed with the Sixth Army Band at the Presidio, and he met Pierre Monteux, the conductor of the San Francisco Symphony. Previn was admitted to Monteux's small conducting class. Previn said, 'Monteux was a marvellous gentleman, a real idol of mine. Something I'll always cherish is that he was the conductor of the London Symphony Orchestra until his death, and four years later I got the orchestra.' Previn had private lessons with Monteux, and was occasionally allowed to conduct a pickup orchestra in rehearsals. While his army buddies were drinking beer in the canteen, Previn studied pocket orchestra scores. He also played chamber music with some of the band musicians. Previn said, 'Some of them were fantastic. I remember a great jazz bassist. The sergeant told him to get a haircut, and he said "I'm hip!" and wound up doing KP.' Previn played piccolo in the band and did band arrangements, including an arrangement of the Shostakovich Fifth Symphony. I asked him how it sounded, and he said, 'Terrible.' In his free time he haunted San Francisco jazz spots, expanding his knowledge and his style in that field. He was never sent overseas, though at one point he received orders to go. Previn said, 'I went to say goodbye to Monteux, on my regular day. Mind you, I was wearing my uniform. I said, "Maître, I won't be able to come for a while, because the army is sending me overseas." He asked where, and I said "Tokyo." Monteux said, "Well, you know, I fell for that once, and that orchestra really isn't good enough." I thought that was lovely.'

Previn stayed on in San Francisco after his two-year term in the army was over, to continue studies with Monteux, and an almost equal amount of time was spent playing jazz. In 1953, 'for reasons of cupidity', Previn returned to Hollywood. For the next decade, he was equally involved with film music and with jazz. Previn said, 'While I was in the army, I met some young men whom I would ordinarily not have met. When they played records, it was very often the kind of jazz I had not heard. After the army, through the kindness of my first wife, whom I had married in 1952, and who is a terrific jazz singer, I got to meet all those players I'd begun to emulate, and I got to play with them. Soon I was in the thick of it – making records, travelling with a trio. Shelly Manne and Red Mitchell were in my first trio, but Shelly was so wildly successful that he didn't have time to travel much, so we got a fine young drummer named Frank Capp. In those days, jazz was in colleges what folk music became later and what, I suppose, certain rock cults are now. So there were jazz concerts *always* in every university – a source of pleasure and very good income for jazz people. I was involved with Jazz With the Philharmonic All-Stars, the Stan Kenton All-Stars – a silly term. If seven people have lunch together, they're immediately the Lunchwagon All-Stars.'

I asked how the famous 'My Fair Lady' jazz album came about, and Previn said, 'We weren't meant to make that. We were just going to record an album – Shelly and Red and I. It was all very laissez faire. We always did jazz records at night. We got to the recording studio, and Shelly wanted to do "On the Street Where You Live". The producer of the record, Les Koenig, suggested that we do the entire score. None of us *knew* it. The show had opened less than a month earlier. There was an all-night record store in LA, so we took a break and had a couple of sandwiches while someone ran out and got it. We listened to it, I wrote out the harmonic changes, and we made it, and we were finished by dawn. We thought it was probably the most expensive "party" record ever made, because who would buy it? If people liked *Fair Lady*, they wouldn't want to listen to it jazzed up, and if people were jazz fans they wouldn't want 'Fair Lady'. And for a couple of years it was the biggest-selling jazz album of all time. It surprised us. We then, typically enough, did eight shows afterward, trying to do it again, without success. Lerner and Lowe told me that they gave that album to the members of the cast for Christmas, which pleased me a lot.' Previn made over sixty solo recordings and records with different combinations of jazz musicians. He added the great jazz trombonist J. J. Johnson to his trio and did an unusual record. 'I wanted to do something with J.J. He was really quite something. A great virtuoso, a good composer, and a wonderful arranger. I suddenly thought of Kurt Weill. He liked that on-purpose seedy sound, which a trombone can certainly provide. It shows in the original orchestrations of *The Three-Penny Opera*. I suggested to Columbia that we do an album of the theatre songs of Weill – the old Berlin ones. They went for it because at the time 'Mack the Knife' was a big hit. Columbia figures that song alone would sell the album. The eight others could be anything I wanted. I wrote some kind of framework arrangements. Neither J.J. nor I knew the tunes in terms of improvising; their harmonic structures were alien to us, and it required some thought. We had a very good time. That album, which probably sold seventeen copies at the time, keeps being reissued, so somebody must like it.'

During the fifties Previn worked with, to name a few, Oscar Peterson, Ray Brown, Herb Ellis, Barney Kessel, Shorty Rogers, Benny Carter, Ben Webster, Art Pepper, Jimmy Giuffre, Dizzy Gillespie, Billie Holiday, Benny Goodman, Buddy deFranco, Frank Rosolino, Russ Freemen, Gerry Mulligan, Peggy Lee, Art Farmer, and he did arrangements for Frank Sinatra, Doris Day and Judy Garland. Previn said, 'The period when I was active in jazz, the fifties – Well, the jazz I admire most today is firmly rooted in that decade. I still have the same heroes. Jazz is an enthusiasm of youth, and you get stuck with the particular era in which you first became interested. When I was active, some people who were, say, twenty years older were still totally entrenched with Benny Goodman. At the time, I didn't understand that, but now the people I still admire are Oscar Peterson, Dizzy Gillespie, Charlie Parker, Lester Young. That's all over now, in terms of the latest word. Some of the new guys go on and on. Keith Jarrett improvises a tune sometimes for forty-five minutes. If you play the piano at all, and you improvise for forty-five minutes, you're bound to come up with *something*. On the other hand, it may be a just criticism to say that I didn't have that *much* to say. I would quit when I thought people listening might think, "That's enough." ' (Red Mitchell once said that most pianists give him an exhausting workout, but that when he played with Previn, after they'd finished he felt like asking, 'What time does the gig begin?' I asked him if that was good or bad. Mitchell thought a second and said, 'I don't know.') Previn said, 'I like jazz people. There's very little political manoeuvring in their lives. They're not subjected to playing with people they don't like. They have two yardsticks: can he play well, and is he a nice fellow? I have good friends in the concert world, but it's not quite as naïvely open as the jazz world. When I played jazz, it consumed a fairly large part of my days, but I did it for fun. I knew it was not forever – certainly not to the exclusion of what I was after. With rare exceptions, I haven't played it in a long time, and not for reasons of misguided disdain. I admire good jazz musicians boundlessly, but I had to figure out which music activities in my life were expendable. I had to let *something* go.'

When Previn stopped working for the Stotharts and the Stolls, and was doing more and more original scores, he gradually became a person to be reckoned with. One of his big achievements was a forty-minute sequence for Gene Kelly's ballet film *Invitation to the Dance*. The film, which had three segments, had been completed, and Kelly didn't like the score he had for a segment based on *La Ronde*, called 'Ring Around the Rosy'. It had been filmed in different locales, and had numerous mood changes. Previn had to fit his score into the finished film – every frame, every nuance. Previn said, 'The dancers were Igor Youskevitch and a ballerina whose name I can't remember. It was a waltz, during which she kept eating. Every time he lifted her, she would eat something before he put her down. Kelly wanted a very romantic waltz, and I wrote one, except the tune was played by tuba and piccolo, accompanied by strings. I thought if I wrote a romantic waltz with the tune played by ridiculous instruments, then

51

it's a double joke.' For that, he was given a special award by the Screen Composers Association. (The other two contributing composers were Jacques Ibert and Rimsky-Korsakov.) Adolph Green said, 'He accepted the compliments modestly and, in effect, said, "Well, that's over with. What's next?" ' Previn worked with Green and Betty Comden on a film, *It's Always Fair Weather*, that got a first-rate critical response, though it wasn't a big success commercially – because, Green says, 'unlike most musicals, it was complex, bitter, sardonic. One song that will someday be recognised was "I Like Myself". André wanted someone to record it, and Sinatra was shooting a picture at the time, so we made an appointment to see him. He had an office in a small building on the lot, along with several actors, including Sidney Blackmer. We went to Sinatra's office at the appointed time – noon – and he wasn't there. We waited around for well over an hour, and Betty said, "He's obviously not coming. We might as well go back to the set." André said, "Well, as long as we're here let's play it for Sidney Blackmer." So typical of him. His genius didn't interfere with his getting along with people. He was just too nice, and completely lacking in the usual horse manure. Anything involving him was discussed rationally. He was too sensible for ego clashes.'

Previn said, 'I liked some of the scores I did – *Elmer Gantry, Bad Day at Black Rock*. I did a score for a movie that was *so* bad it was a classic. Glenn Ford and Ingrid Thulin are lolling around on satin sheets in this palace-like apartment on Avenue Foch, both clearly filthy rich, and it's Nazi-occupied Paris. They're both saying, "Isn't war *hell*?" But I liked my score. Wall-to-wall music. The picture was *Four Horsemen of the Apocalypse*.' (In 1981, Previn was commissioned to write a piece for the Philadelphia Orchestra, which was given its première in Saratoga. One critic was reminded of that old movie score.)

Previn began to get bored writing film scores, because there was so little challenge for him, except for the deadlines, when 'there's not enough time to move the pencil'. He feels that in music, to make a contribution, there should always be some fear. 'The Beethoven Five this week – no matter how many times I do it, I'm scared *witless*. It doesn't matter how many times you conduct a great work. Every single time, you find something new in it.' Previn once precipitated an anxiety attack in himself by setting out to do the near impossible. Musicians were low on the totem pole – they are listed among technicians in the Academy of Motion Picture Arts and Sciences, which caused Aaron Copland to resign – and Previn was somewhat surprised to be invited to Dory Schary's home for a screening of a film Schary needed a score for. Schary was then the head of MGM, and, as was his custom, he served a heavy meal with quantities of wine before the showing, which Previn slept through. When the film ended, the lights came on and Previn woke up. Schary asked him what he thought of it, and Previn said, 'It's terrific!' Schary said that Previn must already have some ideas about the score, and he was interested in hearing what they were. Previn promptly said, 'I'd use just strings. Nothing else.' Schary seemed slightly stunned at that, but said, 'You've got a good track record, so I guess you know what you want.' Previn had the film run for him the second the studio opened the following morning: it was *Designing Woman*, with Lauren Bacall and Gregory Peck. Peck played a newspaper man with Damon Runyon-type friends, and 'all strings' seemed so inappropriate that Previn broke out in a cold sweat. He says now that he rather enjoyed the challenge, working his way out of the corner he'd got himself into, and the completed score was accepted. His other, previous experience with Schary explains why he didn't go to him and say he'd changed his mind about using just strings. Schary had produced *Bad Day at Black Rock*, and had told Previn he wanted lots of French horns in the score. When Previn looked baffled – it was an anti-violence movie, and he couldn't figure out why the producer wanted French horns, lots of them – Schary stood up and mimed pumping a trombone into the air. Previn said, 'Oh, *those* French

53

horns. Ah, yes.' It was a source of almost constant irritation that a producer could complain about something in the score in the same manner in which he might say to the costume designer, 'I don't like those shoes.'

Previn said, 'Naturally, not everyone out there was a fool or a charlatan. I worked with producers and directors I admired enormously. The one I was most fond of was Billy Wilder. He's a wonderfully intelligent and witty and bitter man. His films were terrific – even the ones that weren't commercial hits. If you look at his old films, they're much better than anything that's being done today.'

All told, Previn did over sixty films – not counting two scores that were thrown out because they were too modern. The score for one Bette Davis movie seemed Prokofian to me, and when I mentioned it he laughed and said, 'Absolutely. And in *Four Horsemen* I robbed Shostakovich *blind*.' He summed up all his scores by saying, 'I did a lot of mysteries, and they became a specialty of mine. I did a lot of musicals, and they became a specialty of mine. I did comedies, and they became a specialty of mine. In Hollywood, they *loved* classification. Each time I did something that worked more than once, they said, "Get him for this."' He added, 'Actually, I left at the right moment, because after I left title songs were the big thing, played a hundred times over throughout the film, and I couldn't have written that kind of music. And then the rock groups took over.'

The studio orchestras in Hollywood were 'spectacular', according to Previn. 'They probably still are. The work is steady and the money's good. The best orchestra musicians in the world migrated there. And mixed in with the charlatans were Miklós Rózsa, Alex North, David Raksin. Better than gifted, they were first-rate musicians, and I learned a lot – how to orchestrate better, more quickly. In a way, it beat any conservatory, because I was told to write something, let's say on Monday, and I would hear it played impeccably four days later. So I could stand there with a score and say to myself, "Yes, that's good", or "No, that's not good", or "That you can keep", or "That you must never do again", and so on. In other words, I learned what I was doing wrong. I don't care how many masters look at a score and say, "Don't do that" – it doesn't have the same impact as hearing it.' Previn conducted from a score, not a lead sheet, and he'd learned enough from Monteux to impress those excellent studio musicians, although the first time he conducted a studio orchestra, he was challenged. By mutual preconsent, the musicians tuned to an A-flat. Straight-faced, too, Previn said, 'That's fine. Now, would you all please transpose up a halftone?' The musicians were as bored as Previn was, and they would meet in some high school auditorium or in an empty recording studio for the sheer fun of playing the classics. They often invited Previn to conduct. He said, 'I even got an occasional guest-conducting job with the Los Angeles Philharmonic, and the St. Louis, though they were always pops concerts – Gershwin Night, Rodgers and Hammerstein Night. I began to think more and more about conducting – that it was what I really wanted to do, and it shouldn't be just a hobby.' Previn said that it always takes some catalyst moment to make people move, change things. Considering the gross vulgarities in Hollywood, his moment, in retrospect, seemed almost meaningless. At one point, he was working on a project at Twentieth Century-Fox. 'It was still in the preliminary stages, and the producer – he's dead now, so let's leave him alone – was really not, charitably speaking, terribly intelligent.' During that project, Previn, who is not a drinker, would go home, have a couple, stay up half the night. One day, he was in the producer's office, explaining an idea he had for the music for one scene. The producer didn't understand him. 'I asked him to read the scene, and then we'd discuss it again,' Previn said. 'He opened the script and he read it, and I sat across the room from him and watched, and I noticed that the man moved his *lips* while he read. I thought, "Holy Christ, I'm going home and getting drunk every night because I'm trying to discuss music with a man who moves his lips when he reads." I interrupted him, and said, "I know this sounds insane, and you won't understand it, and I don't want to get in a fight with you, but I'm going home now, and I'm *never* coming back." And I left, and never set foot in a studio again.' But Previn was speaking hyperbolically. He had yet to do two films for which he would get an Academy Award – *My Fair Lady* and *Irma La Douce* – and also *Two for the Seesaw*, *Goodbye, Charlie*, *The Fortune Cookie*, and *The Music Lovers*. For the last, in 1971, Previn recorded the Tchaikovsky music with the London Symphony Orchestra.

CHAPTER 4

A confluence of three men conspired to get Previn out of his rut: Schuyler Chapin, Ronald Wilford, and Roger Hall. And there were three tributaries: William Zalken, Ernest Fleischmann, and Seymour Rosen.

Schuyler Chapin, who is now the dean of the School of the Arts at Colombia University, has been a concert artists' representative; a vice-president in charge of Columbia Records' classical-music division, Masterworks; and the general manager of the Metropolitan Opera during a particularly chaotic period of its history.

After my trip to Pittsburgh, I talked to Chapin, a dark-blond-haired, aristocratic-looking man in his late fifties, about Previn. Everyone I met along the way who knew Previn seemed to be taking his emotional and physical temperature, and Chapin asked, 'How is he? How does he look?' Chapin knew about Previn the jazz player, Previn the film-music composer, and he was truly impressed when he heard the jazz recording of *My Fair Lady* in the fifties. He recognized Previn as 'a man of taste'. He liked some of his film scores, too. Around 1960, when Chapin was with Columbia Records, one of the company's West Coast pops-album producers, Irving Townsend, brought Previn and Chapin together. Previn wanted to do some classical-piano recordings, but at that time Columbia had Rudolf Serkin, Eugene Istomin, Alexander Brailowsky, Gary Graffman, and Glenn Gould under contract. 'It was quite a roster,' Chapin said. At Chapin's invitation, Previn came to New York, and the two had lunch together. Chapin found Previn to be somewhat shy, but with devastating humour. They talked about repertoire, and, as a result, Previn recorded pieces by Hindemith, Roussel, Poulenc and Frank Martin. (When Chapin wants to help someone, he is not only tenacious but bold. He had another idea. Columbia did not have Strauss's 'Burleske' in its catalogue, and he contrived to get Previn to audition for George Szell, a Columbia artist, who was in Los Angeles guest-conducting the symphony there, in the hopes that Previn might record the piece with Szell and the Cleveland Orchestra. Previn said, 'I was thrilled and worried, because Szell was a truly toweringly great musician, but *not* the world's nicest man. I went to his hotel at the appointed time. His suite was so immaculate. Everywhere he worked and lived, whether backstage in his own hall, or in a hotel, there was a kind of "immaculate" that's scary. Not just clean, but *scoured*, almost threatening. He wore rimless glasses that reflected the light and hid his eyes. We sat down, and he asked me endless questions – whether I composed, conducted, whom I'd studied with, played with, all that. Finally, he said, "Well, why don't you play the piece for me?" I was *mightily* relieved, because I was very shy in those days, and didn't have much to say for myself, but I knew I could play the piece. I looked around for a piano, and he said "I do not have a piano here, but I know the piece forwards and backwards. I studied it with Strauss. So just sit down at that table and play it on the table." If it had been anyone else I would have thought he was putting me on. But not George Szell. So I sat down, feeling like the most ridiculous jerk who had ever lived, and started whacking away at the tabletop. After about twenty seconds – the piece opens with a great virtuoso flourish – he stopped me and said, "That's much too slow." At that point, the insanity of the situation got the better of my judgment, and I said, "Well, Maestro, it's because I'm not used to this table. When I play this piece on my table at home, I do it twice as fast." Szell said, "Young man, I don't consider that funny", and the interview was over. When I got home the phone rang and it was Schuyler, calling from New York. He said, "What have you done to Szell?" and I said, "I haven't done a goddam thing to Szell. What has Szell done to *me*?" ' In 1961, Chapin flew to Los Angeles to discuss chamber-music recordings – whatever Previn recorded would have to be something not already in Columbia's catalogue – and while he was there he saw Previn conduct a studio orchestra. Chapin told me, 'You must understand that I have spent my life working with other people's talents. If there's one thing in this world I recognise, it's a talented musician. I watched André working, and the hair on the back of my neck stood on end. After the rehearsal, I had a drink with him, and I asked him, "What do you want to do? If you had your choice, what is your ambition?" And he said, "There's only one thing: I want to conduct. I've wanted to do it all my life." Some gut instinct in me said, "Do something about this." '

It happened that Columbia had a contract with the St. Louis Symphony, and one record remained to be done. The company hadn't intended to pursue it, but this seemed to Chapin a good chance for Previn to 'test the waters'. So Chapin called his friend William Zalken, the manager of the St. Louis Symphony, and asked him to invite Previn to conduct the orchestra and to include in the programmes two pieces that Columbia needed for its catalogue – pieces that, according to Chapin, would make an interesting combination: Aaron Copland's suite from the film score for *The Red Pony* and Benjamin Britten's 'Sinfonia da Requiem'. Zalken, who, it turned out, was as enthusiastic about Previn as Chapin was – he knew Previn well from the times he had conducted pops concerts in St. Louis – agreed. Chapin went to St. Louis for the rehearsals and the concerts, which were a triumph, and the subsequent record was well-received. Chapin said, 'One of the people who noted it was Benjamin Britten. He sent word back: "Who is this fellow André Previn? That's the best performance I've ever heard." '

As Chapin explained, in order to have a career as a conductor Previn would have to have the right manager. Chapin and Zalken both called Ronald Wilford, who at the time was a vice-president of Columbia Artists Management,

America's biggest classical-music management agency. Wilford is now the president. A recent *New York Times* article on the new impresarios – businessmen now, with boards of directors and a keen eye on finances – called Wilford the most powerful man in music in America today. He has a special interest in conductors, and, in the business, he has been called a kingmaker. Chapin felt that Previn was tarred with something that would be difficult to remove – the reputation of being a Hollywood composer and a jazz musician. Wilford, Chapin, and Previn met for lunch at the Plaza, and Chapin says of that meeting, 'It was the first time I realised that under that cool, musing, detached veneer there is a very vulnerable, tense man. I looked across the table at him and realised he was scared green. Wilford told André that it would be a rough go – that if André really wanted to conduct, he would take him on, and book him with every catgut orchestra in the country. He would send him out for a year, and at the end of that year they would both decide whether or not the enterprise was worthwhile.'

That first year, Wilford booked Previn with success by taking advantage of Previn's drawing power as a film-jazz personality and using his talent as a classical pianist. Sometimes Previn would play a Mozart or a Mendelssohn concerto; conducting from the keyboard. He was allowed to choose the balance of the programme. He got an occasional reputable orchestra by filling in at the last minute when a conductor was sick. And he was undergoing the best training imaginable. A first-rate orchestra plays well. The kind of orchestras that Previn was conducting needed to be told how to play – to be taught the music – so Previn had to have strong ideas about what he wanted from an orchestra. (He also made a point of learning to play twelve orchestra instruments – 'miserably', he says – so that he would have an understanding of the musicians' problems. Too many conductors these days – through push or pull, or a combination of both – start at or near the top, and they never really learn their craft. Previn promised himself that he would not conduct pops concerts, but he broke the promise to conduct a benefit programme with the Philadelphia Orchestra. The manager, Roger Hall, called Chapin and said, according to Chapin, 'My God, this guy is fantastic! The orchestra *loved* him I'm going to engage him for a regular-season programme.'

Chapin said, 'Bits and pieces all came together. André was obviously creating a very good impression, getting a good reputation. He was re-engaged by the St. Louis, and I went out to hear the concert. It was the first time I heard him do a Brahms symphony. It sounded just like Furtwängler. I've never heard anything so slow in my life. In point of fact, why shouldn't Previn's Brahms be pontifical and slow? That's what he was brought up on. Mind you, we're talking about him at the very beginning. He was almost diffident then; he didn't want to push. But he began to lose that, because it was obvious that if he was going to have the career he wanted he would have to let his *ego* come to the fore. He would have to push. One of the things that endeared him to managers immediately was that he was the most *economic* rehearsal conductor. He never wastes time. He knows immediately where the problems are and how to correct them.' At the end of the year, Wilford agreed to manage him if Previn would follow his advice. Wilford told him to leave Hollywood, and said he would try to get him an orchestra.

Conductors, managers, recording-company executives move around a lot. Just when you think you have the cast of characters straight, one or another will surprise you by popping up in a different place. Chapin continued to pull strings for Previn. Columbia Masterworks had a strong list of conductors: in addition to Szell, Bruno Walter, Leonard Bernstein, Eugene Ormandy, Thomas Schippers, Igor Stravinsky conducting his own works. It was the early days of stereo, and major repertoire was being re-recorded. Chapin knew that RCA Red Seal had only the Boston Symphony, 'which was not in terribly good shape then'. So Chapin called Roger Hall, who had left Philadelphia to join RCA.

Hall was glad to hear from him. RCA was doing a lot of recording in England then, as many companies do now: America's very strong musicians' union has overpriced its members in terms of recording, and it is cheaper to record in other countries. Just as Chapin and Wilford had used Previn as a pianist to get him into the mainstream of classical music, Hall used other pianists to create a platform for Previn as a conductor, Hall was laying his neck – and RCA's money – on the line. After all, Previn was unknown, and the personal risk for Hall was a big one. The pianists were Lorin Hollander and Leonard Pennario, with the Royal Philharmonic Orchestra. Next, Hall and Wilford approached the managing director of the London Symphony Orchestra, Ernest Fleischmann (he is now the executive director of the Los Angeles Philharmonic). Fleischmann, a musician himself, had been bowled over by Previn's 'My Fair Lady' album, and agreed to a recording session with Previn and the LSO in the summer of 1965. Previn liked the LSO and its members liked him, and he was invited back in 1966, to conduct concerts and to make what was a landmark recording of the Rachmaninoff Second Symphony, inasmuch as he resurrected it: it had been ignored by other conductors for many years. When Hall took a chance on Previn, it was a stroke of genius. Previn's records were fresh and had a spontaneity often lacking in recorded performances. Of this, Previn says, 'The atmosphere of recordings is as unconcertlike as you can get – all the machinery and that red light. It's very restricting. With my funny background – all that work in the studios, on recording stages, which very few conductors have done – when that red light goes on, that's my *night*-light, my security.'

Previn is one of the world's great interpreters of English music. His understanding of that music, and his love for it, began several years after he arrived in Los Angeles. He heard a recording of the William Walton Viola Concerto,

and was so thrilled by it that he began haunting record
stores for more recorded English music, and he also sent
abroad for scores. When he went to England, he had a
sense of déjà vu, a sense that this was where he belonged.
In addition to the Rachmaninoff, Previn recorded the
William Walton First Symphony, also with the LSO, and
the record was so superb that many English critics thought
it was superior to Sir Malcolm Sargent's, one of Walton's
premier interpreters. The success of the Walton prompted
Hall to get Previn to do all nine of the Vaughan Williams
symphonies. When Previn was being 'hounded around
the provinces by Wilford', as he put it, he had conducted
the Houston Symphony, whose conductor was Sir John
Barbirolli. In 1966, Barbirolli resigned, to spend more time
with another orchestra he was in charge of – the Hallé
Orchestra, in Manchester, England. He recommended
Previn to the Houston board, and Previn signed a two-
year contract. There were rumours at the time that Wilford
had feared that Previn would become so firmly established
in England that he would settle there permanently. As it
happens, Previn bought his Surrey country home in 1967,
and, for practical reasons, he got a manager in London,
Jasper Parrott, who co-ordinates the scheduling of all his
European engagements and books his concerts there.
(While Previn was in Houston, two records that he had
made in the early sixties were released by RCA Victor. The
first was a recording he did with the violinist Erick
Friedman, a protégé of Heifetz's, of the Franck and the
Debussy Sonatas. In general, the record was well-received.
One critic wrote, 'There's a youthful, ardent spirit in the
collaboration of violinist Erick Friedman and pianist André
Previn in César Franck's Sonata in A and Debussy's
Sonata in G-Minor. Close rapport between the two is also
evident, a give-and-take where each knows his forward
and receding positions.' Another wrote, 'Thirty years
separate the composition of these two works, the most
powerful and most original French examples of the violin
and piano sonata. No two more talented musicians could

have been selected by RCA than Previn and Friedman to do full justice to these sonatas.' But a third wrote, 'Both Franck and Debussy are hemidemisemigods for Hollywood and pop arrangers. Previn brings every last ounce of rhythmic body English to bare, and Friedman seems willing to go along. Between the slides and smears of his playing and Previn's 86-proof style of barroom rubato these two sonatas are left on their backs like a pair of strangled parakeets.' Previn says, 'That was a *terrible* record. It only stayed in the catalogue about fifteen minutes.' The second record was 'André Previn All Alone'. Previn had gone into a recording studio and, in under two hours, improvised on twenty numbers, and then selected the twelve he liked the best for the album. A lot of critics, and record buyers, too, were pleased to hear him 'all alone'. Some critics said his playing was rich enough not to need any backup, and one noted, 'While his pensive probings honor the melody, he gives added dimension with such ingenious and sensitive harmonic devices as playing in the key of F with his left hand in "Dancing on the Ceiling", while gently stating the melody with his right hand in C.') Previn and Houston – the board, not the orchestra – weren't happy with each other, and by mutual agreement the contract was not renewed. While Previn was in Houston, he was offered the LSO – a proposal that was backed by Wilford and included a lot of recordings – and Previn accepted. He was in a happy position; the orchestra liked him and he was already known in England through his records.

Early in his tenure with the LSO, Previn startled the orchestra and earned the musicians' respect, too. The orchestra played at the Brighton Festival, and on the programme Previn played the Mendelssohn Concerto in G-Minor and conducted from the keyboard. He says, 'Somewhere in the second movement, I had the kind of memory loss which, thank God, is very unusual for me. It was the kind where – it isn't "What's the next bar?" It's "What *piece* am I playing?" It's as if a great door clanged shut. All I knew was that somewhere pretty soon the cellos were going to come in and they were in B-major. So I tried to fix the orchestra with a fairly steely look, which meant "Don't play", and I improvised Mendelssohn-type things, and modulated my way through to a nice F-sharp seventh chord. I then looked at the cellos, gave them a pleading look, and got into B-major. They came in, and when I heard the first note I knew exactly where we were. One local pianist came backstage after the concert and asked what edition I used. Some of the orchestra members heard him, and cracked *up* laughing.'

Seymour Rosen – or Sy, as all his friends call him – met Previn for the first time in the early fifties. Rosen, a tall man with brown hair and quizzical eyebrows and a manner hinting at anticipation and solution of all the problems an orchestra manager encounters, says, 'André was playing with a jazz trio at the Embers, which was a club on Fifty-second Street. I was the bass player with Stan Freeman's trio. I went to hear André, and he was sensational – possibly, because of his training, not quite as free as some players but still sensational. Fifteen or sixteen years later, he came to Pittsburgh, where I was the managing director, to guest-conduct a couple of concerts. When he rehearsed the Pittsburgh, my reaction was very much the same as the orchestra's – underwhelmed. In 1974, we were quietly looking for a music director. William Steinberg, the music director at the time, was very sick – too sick to continue indefinitely – and we were using lots of guest conductors to take some of the load off him. Steinberg was revered, and we didn't intend to break with him. He was an institution. A great Middle-European conductor whom everybody loved. An old-fashioned music director who lived with his orchestra and loved it. We were working with two other conductors. Both gave us heavy amounts of time, and one of them I favoured – an American. But the more he conducted, the more he dug his grave. *Nothing* was happening musically. The other, a European, I didn't consider right for an American

65

orchestra. I was talking to Wilford about guest conductors for the '74–'75 season, and he suggested that we take André Previn for two weeks. I said, "Oh, come on, Ron. That's not for us. I have little respect for him as a conductor." Ron said "When's the last time you saw him?" and I said, " '67". Wilford said, "Well, you ought to see him now. You've got a sick music director, and André sells tickets." To make a long story short, he came and he was wonderful. The weekend concerts were tremendous. We had two truly great weeks. We had one concert in Charleston, West Virginia. André was going to play a Mozart concerto, and the piano was terrible. It had a bad E-flat, and the concerto was in C-minor. You know how crucial E-flat is in that key – the third in the C-minor triad. He had to find a way to play around that note, and he did. He absolutely wowed the orchestra. Members came to me praising him. Especially Fritz Siegal, who said, "That's your boy, Sy." I drove André to the airport, and on the way I said, "I'm going to ask you a question that I have no right to ask. But I need your answer before I can officially ask the question. How would you feel about being our music director?" ' The two talked about the pros and cons for Previn, and he ended up saying to Rosen, 'Call Ron Wilford and tell him I'm more than a little interested.' (Previn told the story slightly differently on the first 'Previn and the Pittsburgh' programme: he said that Rosen had asked him how he would like to have an American orchestra? 'This orchestra?' and that if he had been driving the car they would have gone off the road.) In the spring of 1974, after several talks with the search committees of the board and the orchestra, Rosen and Wilford flew to London to see Previn. 'Upon returning,' Rosen says, 'I announced to the board that Mr Steinberg and I wanted Previn as the next music director. The board vote was one short of unanimous. André really turned the town on. They were the most exciting times Pittsburgh had known in many years. He's tremendously charismatic – he *radiates* on that podium. Pittsburgh, Tanglewood,

Chicago – wherever he is. There are other conductors who play and compose, but they don't do as many things as brilliantly as André does. He's a true Renaissance man. If he has a fault, it's that his genius gets in his way. He's fluent with words and music, and he can be glib. At times, I think there is something stopping André Previn from *being* André Previn. I don't know what it is. I think one day, if André can get through to himself, let himself show, he will really be the greatest conductor of the twentieth century.'

Elden Gatwood, who joined the Pittsburgh in 1963 – he had been second oboe in the Cleveland for ten years, and left when he could no longer tolerate George Szell and was offered the first chair in Pittsburgh – says, 'The Pittsburgh was in total chaos in 1975. There was *no* communication between the orchestra and management. Hostility in the orchestra was rampant. Previn had to overcome the orchestra's suspicions, and he was besieged with small problems. But Previn is very accessible, and I'm pleased with his musicianship, his approach to ensemble in the orchestra, and with the new members that have been hired since his arrival. The quality of the orchestra has never been better. Some audience members found Previn's conducting style unexciting and cancelled their subscriptions. Steinberg had conducted with a great deal of abandon, arms flying, and let the orchestra play the way it felt. He didn't care very much about balance – at least not during the time that I was here. Steinberg doubled everything in German pieces – Brahms, Beethoven. Four woodwinds instead of two, four of this, four of that. We played very big. Previn never doubles anything. He wants transparency, more reserve, control. The critics made unfair, negative comparisons with Steinberg, because Steinberg was what they'd become used to.'

A lot of people in Previn's life are hurt by his behaviour – warm and friendly one minute, cold and remote the next. Chapin, who is the twins' godfather, says that in all his years in the business he's never met anyone as totally involved with music as Previn is, and he said recently, 'André is an extraordinarily well-rounded, decent, good human being, but that is not always immediately discernible. We sometimes expect intimacy on the basis of the fact that almost every time he performs he moves us, touches us, gives us a feeling of self, and the world, and the soul. It's axiomatic in my experience that *all* performers suffer from this imposed problem. We expect them to respond to our needs, rather than our responding to their needs. Talented human beings who deliver so much to us are expected to do the same, and even more, in private. They're not the same in private. There's no reason they should be. In his working life, André is always putting out. He *has* to withdraw to survive.'

Chapin went on to say, 'André is a very complicated fellow, obviously. A year or so ago, he was at our house one night for dinner. Just my wife and I and one of our children. We were talking music, and he went to the piano to illustrate a point. He always has a kind of hunted, haunted look. Very rarely is his facial expression relaxed. He said, "It's supposed to go like this, but most people do this." As he was playing, I looked at his face, and all of a sudden every bit of pain was gone. It was the face of a man deeply content. A little half-grin. After he'd finished, he looked around for a bit, then stayed and played for ten minutes or so, and I thought, "My God, this is the only time that that man is ever truly happy – when he is making music." All that weight, whatever it is, those demons go away. In his own quiet way, he's absolutely beatific. He finished playing and sort of smiled, and right away back came the other part. I've never forgotten it. When he is sitting at the piano, or conducting, that is when he is a complete person.'

Chapin has helped many a musician, but he can't, offhand, recall anyone but Previn not only being grateful for his help but publicly acknowledging it, too. He has got pleasure from watching Previn's progress, which has not surprised him, since in his view Previn is 'skilful, committed, communicative, passionate about music, and – that rarity in conductors – modest.' Chapin adds that Previn is a true musician, in the sharing of musical responsibilities and joys. The happiest day he spent with Previn was in 1976, when he was in London on business. His last day there, he went to Surrey, around noontime, to see Previn. Chapin says, 'We sat in his living-room and did not budge. We just talked. It was marvellous and relaxed. The phone rang a few times – calls about his programme in Berlin, a programme in Vienna – and every time he hung up he would say, "I still can't believe this." '

One thing Previn remembers of this period is an appearance in London on a radio talk show called 'Desert Island Discs'. Guests were asked to name a book they would want if they should be stranded on a desert island, excluding the Bible and Shakespeare, which would already be on the island. Previn said he would like a book on how to build a boat. Near the end of the programme, the interviewer asked Previn, as he asked other guests, what he would like if he could have anything he wanted. Previn said that he would like to be the music director of the London Symphony Orchestra – 'something beyond my wildest dreams'. A short time later, he got it. Previn is full of praise for Ronald Wilford. On the day that we talked in his apartment, he said, 'Many people find Ron difficult, even abrasive – at least when it comes to business matters. He's always been wonderful to me – truly concerned, caring. And he's an absolute wizard in the business. He'd say, "Don't programme Mozart or Haydn in City X. They won't like it", or "No choral works in City Y. They don't have a good chorus." I did mostly standard repertoire. I was still learning.' He laughed, and added, 'I still am. In that trial year, I stayed in more Holiday Inns than I can count, and worked for fees that didn't cover my expenses. I think audiences came assuming that it would be a pops concert. By the time they noticed that it was Beethoven, it was too late. The doors were locked. I didn't care. After all, you only get one turn in this life.'

Previn has said that some critics in the States will forgive a conductor anything, including a long prison term. Anything but composing Hollywood film scores. When I asked if he had been well received, had got good reviews, he said, 'Oh, God Almighty, *no*! Oh, my God! There were certain reviews – you have no *idea* how terrible they were. Jesus!' He burst out laughing, 'But, unlike actors who can still quote the bad review they got in Bellows Falls, Vermont, in 1938, I can't do that for you. You see, when you're starting out and you get an absolute *wipeout* bad review, you always get terribly hurt. Now, with enough years of retrospection, it seems very likely that I deserved them. I was probably simply not good enough to do the things that I had the temerity to do.' (Previn edited, and wrote the introduction to, the book *Orchestra*, a collection of interviews with orchestra players – and ex-players – from all over the world. In the chapter on players' opinions and descriptions of conductors, there is no mention of Previn. In another section of the book, however, an LSO player is quoted as saying of Previn, 'He often came ill-prepared.') Previn said, 'The reviews might have been absolutely justified. The point is, if I had said, "OK. You don't want me. I won't do it anymore", then I would not have the right to call myself a musician, because you don't do it for somebody on a paper. So if I have got enough better to have convinced *some* of them that it's now worth listening to, that's fine. At the time, you always think, "How ugly of them. How unjust." But later on, you think, "Well, what if they were right?" At first, every review began with "Last night, Hollywood's André Previn. . ." and I could have dictated the rest of the review. I stopped reading them. They were uniformly dreadful. The first time I got a review that didn't mention Hollywood in the first sentence, I felt I'd made it. The review was *terrible*, but I could get down to the business of correcting what was wrong. Critics in this country write reviews that are in the nature of a news bulletin that says, "Last night, X played, and he's no good." You can't review any artistic endeavour in the same language as "Last night the drugstore on the corner of Fourth and Main burned down", because that's a *fact*. You can go and look at the *rubble*. But you can't say this pianist, this singer, this conductor is no good, because it's not a *fact*, it's an opinion. Of course, to be the devil's advocate, the fact that a critic is allowed a byline automatically makes it an opinion. On the other hand, Ashkenazy got a terrible review the last time he gave a concert in New York, and it is simply not *possible* for him to play that badly. Critics can be extremely helpful or extremely harmful, peripherally, to a career. But they do not make or break people. They *can* make them move. Claudia Cassidy, in Chicago, thought Jean Martinon was lousy. That's her prerogative. He was a *superb* conductor and a wonderful musician. There were certain areas of the repertoire he wasn't comfortable in, but I don't know anybody who is comfortable in everything. She kept at him until his *ulcers* couldn't take it. In London, after you have made certain inroads in the musical life and they know you're going to return often, if they don't like a performance they tend to write that you had a bad night, that it wasn't as good as on a certain other occasion, and that they are looking forward to. . .et cetera. There are certain people in England in the writing profession who've helped me a lot, and I'm grateful to them, but I don't think I'd have given up if they'd all hated me. Nor would I have become complacent if they had all loved me.'

Previn tends to understate his accomplishments as a composer, and he seems to require a deadline to actually get around to composing. He did the score for the Broadway musical about Chanel, *Coco*, with Alan Jay Lerner. In Lerner's autobiography, *The Street Where I Live*, he says of Previn, 'One day we were sitting together discussing the kind of song required for a particular scene. As we talked, our conversation being punctuated from time to time with a non-sequitur story or a bit of humour, André seemed to be doodling. Suddenly he rose from his chair and handed me a piece of paper containing the doodling. It was a complete piano part for a song which he had composed during our conversation. There would be no point to this story if it were a bad song, but it happened to be a very good one and became one of the highlights of the play.' Previn would like to collaborate with Lerner again someday, if the project was right.

Previn also collaborated with Tom Stoppard. Previn initially suggested something for narrator and orchestra, but Paul Scofield in a dinner jacket didn't appeal to Stoppard. Then Previn suggested a play with actors, and with the symphony orchestra playing a role. After several months had passed, Stoppard called with an idea. He told Previn that it was not basically amusing, and it might be impossible to stage. Previn said, 'He sent me a first draft, and I was so crazy about it I said, "Why don't we write it, and worry later about how to stage it?" And that's what we did. The result was *Every Good Boy Deserves Favour*. It's about a man who, for political reasons, has been put in a Russian insane asylum. His cellmate is *truly* crazy, and thinks there is a symphony orchestra in the cell with him. The orchestra plays very often in the man's deranged mind. The doctor – the analyst – is an amateur violinist, who, for fun, plays in an amateur orchestra. And we started confusing things by having the doctor get up from the orchestra and put the fiddle down to go to his office. It was performed at Her Majesty's Silver Jubilee, for a festival that I was in charge of. Trevor Nunn directed it with actors from the Royal Shakespeare. We thought we were going to put it on once. To our surprise, it was an enormous success, and since then it's played in about twelve languages, all over the world. I'm pleased for Tom. Because of *EGBDF*, he's been banned from Russia. I thought that was lovely.' Previn, too, was banned from Russia, though he doesn't volunteer the information. The score brilliantly emulates Shostakovich and Prokofiev. (In

1979, *EGBDF* had a run at the Metropolitan Opera House. The producer wanted Previn to conduct opening night, but Previn, who has said he feels like a ventriloquist when someone else conducts his works, refused, because David Gilbert, the regular conductor, had done 'the dogsbody work and deserves all the credit'.)

Previn wrote a commissioned piece for the Pittsburgh Symphony which was designed, as the title, *Principals*, indicates, to show off the principals in each section. He donated his fee to the orchestra's instrument fund. He had recorded a lot of Prokofiev just before he wrote the piece, and he said, '*Every* critic is going to find it derivative.' He was pleased to be commissioned to write a piece for the Philadelphia Orchestra and one for the Vienna Philharmonic. In 1975, he composed a piano suite for Ashkenazy, which the pianist has 'taken around the world', to great acclaim, and Ashkenazy is looking forward to performing a piano concerto that Previn is now completing. Previn wrote a song cycle for Dame Janet Baker, which has also been well received. And the jazz tunes he wrote and embellished for Itzhak Perlman – illustrating his understanding of the violin and the graceful use of all that instrument's possibilities in the hands of a consummate artist – suggest that a violin concerto should be on his agenda.

When Previn was a child in Berlin he practised the piano every day after school. Often he heard his father come home, his arrival announced by the sound of his keys being dropped on a metal cover on a radiator. More times than not, Previn's father would open the door to the music room, stick his head in, and say one word: '*Falsch!*' ('Wrong!') I asked Previn how his father, who died in 1963, felt about the Hollywood and jazz periods, and about his conducting.

Previn said, 'He didn't understand jazz, and he never considered the Hollywood work a permanent thing. He was somewhat ambivalent. If I was composing, I should be conducting. If I was conducting, I wasn't conducting the right composers. It had to be Beethoven or Brahms. I always tried to get my father's approval, and if, secretly, I had it he would not admit it. When I finally committed myself to conducting, I think he was pleased. There was one early season that was quite impressive. There were a lot of second-rate orchestras, of course, but, to my surprise, there were quite a few first-rate ones. I called my father and rather boastfully read him the list, hoping to impress him. There was a long pause, and then he said, "You can't get Boston, can you?"

Part II

CHAPTER 1

Tanglewood, the summer home of the Boston Symphony Orchestra and the Berkshire Music Center, is a pastoral paradise for musicians – over two hundred acres cradled in the Berkshires, in western Massachusetts, near the towns of Lenox and Stockbridge. Previn says of Tanglewood, 'There are a lot of summer festivals, and most are either to keep the orchestra lucratively busy, to meet the payroll, or they are a desperate attempt to draw huge audiences. Granted, the BSO is one of the greatest symphonies in the world. Its musicians have to be kept busy, of course, and they would love it if every night were jammed full. But that is only fifty per cent of Tanglewood. The other fifty per cent is working with the absolute cream of music students from all over the world. And I find that it is that kind of division of labour that makes Tanglewood so wonderful. To walk around and hear students practising, to know that the rehearsals are *full* of music students, of conducting students with scores, eyes *riveted* to the page. So serious, and so ambitious. They *care* so much. I find it absolutely wonderful. To me, it's thrilling to conduct the Boston, but working with the student orchestra and the student conductors is *just* as big a reason for me to come to Tanglewood. I'm not happy working summers, but this is a genuine exception. I'll always come here if they ask me.'

Previn has been one of a number of visiting conductors at Tanglewood – at the invitation of Seiji Ozawa, the Boston Symphony music director, and Gunther Schuller, the artistic director of the Berkshire Music Center. Leonard Bernstein is always welcome, and usually there. Previn enjoys Tanglewood so much that one summer he figuratively broke his neck to get there. He says, 'I was conducting in Salzburg, and the day after the last concert I

77

had to get to Tanglewood. I arrived at the airport at nine in the morning, only to learn that my flight had been cancelled, and the next plane would leave that night. I was not prepared to sit on my luggage for twelve hours – that airport has about three minutes' entertainment value. So I went to the counter and asked, "Where does the next flight go?" "Zurich." I thought, "Good. The Zurich airport is bigger, and there are more flights." So I took the scores I needed, my razor, toothbrush, and a shirt, and put them in a bag, which I carried on to the plane. I knew I wouldn't be seeing the luggage for a while. When I got to Zürich, I asked if they had a flight to Boston. No. New York? No. "Well, where can you get me right away?" "Amsterdam." "Fine." In Amsterdam, I asked if they had a flight to New York. No. Boston? Yes. *Great*! In Boston, I caught a plane to Pittsfield, and in Pittsfield I rented a car and drove to Stockbridge and the Red Lion Inn, where I usually stay. I felt as if I'd been through three wars, but I got there.'

The Boston Symphony holds its rehearsals and concerts in Tanglewood's Music Shed, a rough-hewn structure that was completed in 1938. Eero Saarinen had a hand in its design. Lack of funds was the initial reason for the unfinished interior, but the acoustics proved to be so good that, with a few exceptions, including kite-shaped grey acoustical panels in flight formation which cover the ceiling's steel girders above the orchestra, nothing has been changed. The Shed is wedge-shaped, curved at the broad end, and open on three sides. The roof extends beyond the seating area, and, as one visitor puts it, 'the music comes out and the rain doesn't get in'. Five thousand slatted wood seats fan out from the stage, and are divided into nineteen sections, separated by wide aisles and white steel pillars, which have the section numbers painted on them high and in huge numerals, for easy identification. Outside, on each side of the Shed, there are rows of long green benches to accommodate the music students and off-duty volunteers who work at Tanglewood as ushers. People who do not have reserved seats sit on the lawn. They bring blankets, chairs, food, and wine, and it is not unusual to see evening dress and candelabras, too.

On a Wednesday morning in July, Previn arrived early for the ten o'clock rehearsal. He would have two three-hour rehearsals Wednesday and Thursday for the Friday and Saturday concerts: on Friday the orchestra would play the Elgar 'Enigma' Variations and the Rachmaninoff third piano concerto, with Horacio Gutiérrez as soloist, and on Saturday the Haydn Symphony No. 88 and the Mahler Symphony No. 4, with the soprano Kathleen Battle. Not nearly enough rehearsal time, but, as Previn says, 'this orchestra is run off its *feet* during the season'. On the following Friday, Previn would conclude his stay at Tanglewood by playing the Mozart Piano Quartet in G-Minor, K.478, with members of the Boston Symphony, for the seven-o'clock Weekend Prelude concert.

Previn was wearing a navy-blue T-shirt, jeans and blue jogging shoes, and he had a khaki jacket tossed over one shoulder, though Tanglewood was having a heat wave. He talked to Joseph Silverstein, the leader and a good friend, whom he calls Joey; spoke to several other friends in the orchestra; and, promptly at ten, started the rehearsal. The stage was mercilessly hot, but the audience area had the benefit of morning breezes. One or another section of the grass that stretches from the Shed, at the eastern edge of the lawn, to the Theatre-Concert Hall, at the western edge, is perpetually being mowed, and the breezes were scented with a lovely blend of pine, from the grove of trees that backs the Shed and half encircles it, and new-mown grass.

There was a sizable number of students at the rehearsal, many following scores, and a general air of informality. Previn's relationship with the Boston Symphony, unlike the ones with the London Symphony Orchestra and the Pittsburgh Symphony, is almost businesslike. Because he is a guest conductor, a certain degree of formality carries over even to the rehearsals. (He did surprise, and perhaps warm up, the Boston his first summer there, though. He was asked to do, among other things, the Rachmaninoff second symphony, and at a rehearsal he stopped conducting at the end of the clarinet solo in the third movement and said to the soloist, Harold Wright, 'My God! That is the most beautiful thing I have ever heard in my life.') Some London Symphony members, on the other hand, recall rehearsals when they laughed almost more than they played. Previn hopes this is true, because he feels that making music is so deadly serious, such a matter of life and death, that levity is a necessary relief.

The Tanglewood rehearsals were succinct. Previn had only an hour and a half with Gutiérrez, but they both accepted this philosophically, and the performance went superbly. Miss Battle, a beautiful young black woman, proved to have the floating, rounded, almost unearthly sound that is perfect for Mahler. At both concerts, Previn, in white jacket (because of the heat the orchestra men played in white shirts, the women in white blouses), was, to the audience, a magnet on the podium. At each performance, there was a near-capacity crowd; the Shed was filled, and there were some seven thousand people on the lawn. The often acerbic Richard Dyer, of the Boston *Globe*, reviewing the first concert, was almost beside himself with praise. Dyer did not review the Haydn-Mahler concert, but Stefan Kozinski, one of the student conductors, whom I'd talked to several times during rehearsal breaks – *he* was riveted to the scores – told me at summer's end how he felt about it. Kozinski had studied at Princeton and Juilliard, and had spent a year and several summers studying with Nadia Boulanger in France, and he had wooed his wife with Previn's recording of Rachmaninoff's Second Symphony. Of Saturday night's concert, he said, 'In the Mahler, there was a very personal warmth coming from Previn. It is human love, and you know he is terribly involved, really baring himself – a great difficulty for many conductors. It's a highly transcendental piece – a glimpse into the other world that Mahler was yearning for. The third movement, in particular, was the peak of the month, if not the entire season – the million-dollar moment at Tanglewood. All of the sudden pianissimos were great, but there was one in particular that was wonderfully structured, planned, by Previn. There were certain moments – a new phrase, a progression – where you heard the silence along with the music. The only unfortunate aspect of the Mahler was that it made people forget the Haydn 88. It was considered a *prelude* to the Mahler by everyone – even people in the trade. They were two marvellous achievements of human history. They coexisted.'

Directly in front of the main gate, and midway into the Tanglewood grounds, is the Main House of the Berkshire Music Center – a rambling green building, encircled by a porch, where student chamber-music groups are coached by members of the Boston Symphony and visiting musicians. There are small studios edging the lawn, but the lawn itself is a grand sweep of greenery, punctuated by an occasional old and stately spruce or chestnut. Just inside the gate, to the right, is a gift shop, and to the right of that is a cafeteria for students and concertgoers. Down a dirt path from the cafeteria is the Theatre-Concert Hall, where Previn worked with the student orchestra and two of the conducting fellows on Monday, Tuesday, and Wednesday, for a Wednesday-night concert. (Of the twenty students in this year's conducting seminar, four had received fellowships, which meant, among other things, that they could conduct the student orchestra on a regular basis.) The hall, which seats eleven hundred, is every bit as rustic as the Music Shed. It is enclosed on three sides, however, and there are several corrugated-steel doors that can be pulled down to enclose the forth side – the back – in bad weather.

I had coffee with Previn in the cafeteria before the ten-o'clock rehearsal on Monday, and he told me something about the Vaughan Williams Symphony No. 5, which he would conduct. 'It took living in England a long time for me to understand how to do his music. The, if you like, *sentiments* expressed in it are not very overt, and often orchestras other than English ones, or orchestras with conductors who have not spent a great deal of time with English music, superimpose the kind of espressivo on it that is used in Tchaikovsky, and it won't work. It's simply not that kind of sentiment. It has to be left alone, and it will make its point by itself. I think it was Peter Warlock who said of one of the Vaughan Williams symphonies that it was like a cow looking at you over a gate. Very beautiful, but so what? That's very *funny*, but it's not true. What I hope to show these kids – and it's easier with kids, because they haven't got that precedential playing yet – is that the simpler the music is played, and the less the personal emotion involved, the more the piece pays off. It might take a while to get the strings not to lean *into* it, in that kind of Russian and/or American style of playing that strings have – simply to let the music happen by itself. That symphony, in particular, of all his nine, is the one I like the best. It's the *least* dramatic.'

Shortly before ten, Previn went down the dirt path to the hall. The student-orchestra members were unpacking their instruments in the front rows of the auditorium. Some were already onstage. The student conductors were scattered through the audience, scores in laps. In addition to the Vaughan Williams, the programme would consist of Richard Strauss's 'Don Juan', conducted by Jahja Ling, from Jarkarta, and Mozart's Symphony in A-Major No. 29, led by another young man, who, charitably, will not be named. Gustav Meier, the coordinator of the conducting programmes and the chief coach, was onstage, seated to the right, and Previn joined him. Throughout the rehearsals, Previn and Meier sat there and observed the two conducting fellows. The orchestra members were young. The leader, who had curly brown hair and hazel eyes and was dressed in shorts, T-shirt, and sandals – the rehearsal uniform for most of the musicians, for the heat wave had

82

not abated – appeared to be in his late teens. The ages of the others ranged from eighteen to twenty-eight.

Using a score, Jahja Ling, a thin young man with straight black hair and wire-rimmed glasses, wearing slacks and a sports shirt, led the orchestra through a reading of 'Don Juan' with a sensitivity and eagerness that were almost tangible. He was openly grateful for playing that pleased him, smiling radiantly at times. He was polite, and requested rather than demanded certain things of the musicians. After he had finished, he talked to Meier and Previn about various points in the piece, noting in his score details to be attended to at another rehearsal. The other conducting fellow led the Mozart with windmill arms, no baton. There were knee bends and verbal orders: 'Loud', 'Soft', 'Short', 'Long', 'More', 'Less'.

During a break, when almost everyone hurried up the dirt path to the cafeteria for something to eat, Previn stood outside the hall, drinking a Coke he'd got from a backstage vending machine. I asked if the gymnastic gestures we had just witnessed were appropriate for anything, and Previn said wryly, 'Possibly *Elektra*.' (The Mozart conductor had begun the symphony with a gesture suitable for stopping traffic; and before one rehearsal one of the student conductors asked Previn how *he* would start it. At first, Previn demurred, saying 'That's really not fair.' But the student persisted, and Previn demonstrated: a minute downbeat, a nod. And he said, 'Mind you, it took me about ten years to learn that.')

Back in the hall, Previn mounted the podium and began the Vaughan Williams. In one section, the opening bars were sustained triple pianissimo, and he held the first note and, with his left hand, brought the players down to just a whisper. He said, 'That's what I want. Sensational. Really sensational.' Of a horn passage, Previn said, 'You don't need me there. I'll stand here and try to look busy.' The musicians applauded. 'The forte at Seven – can the horns be really extreme? And *hold* it.' Several bars later: 'No, no. Start your decrescendo sooner. . . Oh, *yes*', with

83

pleasure. During a woodwind solo: '*Hear* what's going on, and adjust. It's not enough to look at the score and the conductor.' Of a passage that wasn't articulated to his satisfaction: 'That won't happen again, so we don't have to go over it. Let's go on.' And 'Before Nine, the two eighth notes – don't think of them as just two notes on their way to a downbeat. They're important.' In the third movement, he asked the leader if he would like to do his solo again, and the young man nodded. After he'd played it, Previn said, 'Bravo', and again the orchestra members shuffled their feet. Before another triple-pianissimo passage, he said, 'At this point, we have to take all the glue off the notes. The melody is sentimental enough. We don't have to add to it. A little less vibrato, please, and the notes not so sustained.'

Previn has said that private teaching is not something he likes to do, but he's good at working with groups of young musicians, and is always encouraging. He was low-key, sometimes amusing, during the rehearsal. At one point, a flute player missed an entrance. Previn stopped and said, 'I paid you a compliment and you double-crossed me. I once asked Jimmy Galway why he quit the Berlin Philharmonic. He said, "I just got tired of being pointed at." So I didn't point at you. And you didn't come in.' Out on the lawn, a baby was crying. Previn said, 'Does that belong to one of you? No? Let's proceed. Before you play one *note* in the third movement, make a mental note that it is already too loud.' There was an English-horn solo in that movement, and before it began Previn told the orchestra a joke. 'There was a horn player in the LSO who *never* missed an entrance. He said to me, "I might not play the right notes, but I always come in." I bet him five pounds that I could *make* him come in at the wrong time. I'd noticed that he usually waited until his solo was coming up before he stopped reading a book, or whatever, to look at me. I could see his lips moving, counting bars: "Forty-five, forty-six, forty-seven." This time, when he looked at me I mouthed, "Fifty-one, fifty-two, fifty-three",

84

and he absolutely *plunged* in, in the wrong place. It *enraged* him, but he paid me the five pounds.' The young musicians, who had not reacted to the Galway anecdote, laughed at this one. Continuing with the music, Previn said, 'Don't *prepare* the triple pianissimo. It should be subito. And here's a blanket rule: when it gets faster, it's not necessarily louder. And it doesn't say so at Ten, but *push* toward the top note.' He sang the phrase to demonstrate, and then said, 'Christ, I sang that out of tune.' As they played, he said to a section or to a principal, without stopping, 'That's very nice', 'Lovely', 'That's really beautiful', 'We have a little work to do on that.' He stopped. 'Since it's so relentlessly pianissimo, the sudden fortes should be short, piercing – shafts of light. And at Fifteen – I don't think that's secure. It's correct, but it doesn't have any conviction. And this is true everywhere – Chicago, Boston: when there's a note tied over the bar, followed by fast notes, everybody rushes the fast notes. Don't do it. It comes up so often – let's get it right. And trumpets, I want to pay you a backhanded compliment: anybody can make mistakes, but not everyone can correct them while *making* them.' The orchestra shuffled applause, and Previn added, 'But don't do it again.' At another point, Previn stopped to say, 'Horns, you're not in tune.' The orchestra's four horns repeated the passage, and again they were not in tune. Previn continued with the rehearsal nevertheless, and the next day the horns were onstage early, practising the difficult section until they got it right.

At the final rehearsal, Previn said, 'I will try not to stop, but if anything bothers you, for God's sake speak up.' He had won them over. They responded to his every gesture, and their playing had a shimmering, pure beauty. There were foot shuffles for a viola solo and again for the leader's solo. About the ethereal, almost silent ending, Previn had instructed the strings to 'give yourself enough bow to make that final note last ten minutes', and the note melted into nothingness.

Previn, still standing on the podium, said, 'I won't have a chance to talk to you tonight, and I want to say that this has been a great pleasure for me. You can play – you can play *anything*. You like to play, you *love* music, and you get pleasure from it. Those things should always be present. Unfortunately, they aren't. If you can, hang on to that.'

To Jahja Ling, who had repeatedly sought Previn's advice on 'Don Juan', Previn said, 'Be bold, be daring, take chances. You might be terrible, you might be absolutely wonderful. But you won't be boring.'

At the concert, Jahja Ling, though he brought the score onstage, conducted without it. The performance was one of the most electrifying 'Don Juan's I'd ever heard, and afterward Ling said, 'The orchestra was so fantastic. They responded to my *eyelashes*.' He was glowing. The young man conducting the Mozart did not shout at the orchestra but confined himself to knee bends and arm flailings. The Vaughan Williams was a miracle of music-making, and at the end the orchestra applauded along with the audience.

CHAPTER 2

Student conductors come to Tanglewood filled with high hopes. They have been specially chosen, in a nine-month, worldwide screening process, and they all know that Tanglewood is where Leonard Bernstein, Seiji Ozawa, Claudio Abbado, Michael Tilson Thomas, Sarah Caldwell, and many others have made their mark. Stefan Kozinski said, 'It's a garden for conductors', but he also said, 'Because of its *hugeness*, success here is not so possible as it once was. The amount of time a young conductor must spend being political is just so much time taken away from the music.' And most of the student conductors find themselves in a frustrating position at Tanglewood. With the exception of the four conducting fellows, they are limited to practising gestures in a room with a mirror and conducting orchestral repertoire played by two pianists, trained in Tokyo and hired by Ozawa. They will possibly be told by Ozawa or Bernstein or a visiting conductor, at a seminar, that if they can't keep two pianists together, how can they expect to succeed with a hundred musicians? Most feel that conducting two pianists is more difficult, and that it's nearly impossible to work up steam in the 'Eroica', singing phrases, gesturing freely, cuing a non-existent oboe in front of their peers and under the close scrutiny of Ozawa or Bernstein, or both. It's hard to imagine their learning anything except, perhaps, poise under fire.

Some conductors – Maurice Abravanel, Erich Leinsdorf, Previn, to name a few – prefer to talk to the students rather than to attempt to teach technique in a limited period of time. Abravanel feels such instruction can be destructive – that in the process of correcting an awkward gesture, creativity can be inhibited. At seventy-seven, he had seen many of the world's greats – Toscanini, Bruno Walter, Monteux – and he talks about their habits and musicianship. To young conductors who might sometimes feel, as many musicians do, that a conductor's role in music is not so important, he says, 'Music is just a skeleton of a work until a conductor puts his own blood into it. Then it becomes a work of art.'

Previn told Gunther Schuller and Meier that he'd like to talk to the young conductors about his experiences, and what they might come up against in a world he himself had been introduced to relatively late in life; and on Thursday afternoon at two Previn, Meier, and the student conductors met at Seranak, which had been the summer home of Serge Koussevitzky, the BSO's music director from 1924 to 1949. The twenty young conductors this summer came from seven states (New York, Ohio, North Carolina, Delaware, Massachusetts, Colorado, and Connecticut) and five other countries (Spain, Brazil, Argentina, Indonesia, and Japan, which supplied five of them). They all had expensive glossy photographs, repertoire lists, and some reviews – for they all had some experience. Jahja Ling, though he had won a bronze medal and a certificate of honour in major piano competitions, wanted to be a conductor, but his accent had not helped him in a bid for an assistantship in Indianapolis, because it was felt he would not speak clearly enough to be understood at children's concerts, which were part of an assistant's duties. All twenty came to the seminar, their heads filled with abstract terms – 'vortex', 'fulcrum', 'rebound' – which would recede in importance in the emotion of really conducting, if they ever got a chance at it. An especially sensitive, hardworking group of musicians, they gave the lie to the cliché notion that most conductors are just standing up there waving a stick, out of some misguided desire for power. (If you ask an orchestra member to name his favourite conductors, he's apt to reply, 'They're all dead.')

Seranak is halfway up Bald Head Mountain, in the

middle of a hundred and seventy acres of Berkshire beauty. It is approached by a winding road that was cut out of the mountainside, and the road threads through maples and is edged with white hydrangeas. Behind a broad terrace outlined with huge pots of red begonias stands a nineteen-room white Newport-style house with a shingle roof, overlooking Tanglewood, an immense lake, and distant blue mountains.

The living-room, where the class met, is dominated by an almost life-size portrait of Koussevitzky, standing, poised to play a bright-orange string bass. There are two grand pianos and an assortment of antique furniture, which had been pushed against the walls to make room for grey metal folding chairs. Previn and Meier shared a Victorian sofa, facing the class. During the afternoon, only two student voices were readily identifiable: Mr Ling, because of his accent, and an attractive young woman from New York named Margery Deutsch, because she was the only woman in the class.

Meier, whom Helen Epstein once described in the *New York Times* as 'a Swiss-born island of sanity' at Tanglewood, brought the class to order by saying, 'Do I have to introduce – ' Applause. 'No, I don't think so.'

Previn said, 'I have no road map for this afternoon. I just thought there must be things that you want to know – on a musical level, a musicological level – which I can't usually answer. Or I can volunteer just cynical professionalism, which is something you'll have to face sooner or later. I didn't even prepare any particular sage opening remarks.'

A young man raised his hand.

Previn said, '*You* came prepared', and the class laughed.

'As a composer, do you trust players to do what you want?' the young man asked. A number of the students were composers as well as conductors.

Previn said, 'Oh, yes. I trust players – if things are written down correctly. It's *me* I don't trust.' Laughter. 'First of all, I'd like to say that I'm a conductor who also composes, not a composer who conducts. My pieces are generally meant to *sound* good. The composing part is backbreaking for me, but I spent so many years in Hollywood orchestrating music for people who couldn't do it that that part is fun. I can do it with the World Series on. But, to get to your question, the matter of trusting players has nothing to do with a 'new' work. I think you'll find that the more you trust the players – whether you're doing a Haydn symphony or something with the ink still wet – the better off you'll be. I have a theory that when you have a new piece, the more complex it is, and the more difficult it is, and the more chances there are of *desperate* mistakes, whether rhythmical accidentals, or a fault of the copyist – some dense thing, like a new piece of Tippett's – the more advisable it is to read a whole movement, or at least half a movement, straight through, disasters and all. It gives the players a chance to know what the piece is likely to be about once it gets corrected. When I was starting out, there was a terrific urge in me to *instantly* stop and correct a wrong note – wrong entry, wrong time, wrong pitch, whatever. But I soon realized that a good player would know in a second what *I* knew, and the next time he wouldn't play it wrong. So, in a way, you're wasting everybody's time if you stop and correct a mistake. The second time through, I would say, at least fifty per cent of the mistakes will have corrected themselves. It will be harder for you to ferret out the remaining mistakes, but easier on the orchestra. So I always trust the players. Not only do I *trust* them. You'll find that very often they will bail you out.' Explosive laughter.

'No, really. Believe me. When I took over the LSO in the late sixties, the principal horn was Barry Tuckwell, and we got to be good friends. He said to me once, "André, when you get lost in a piece – and you will – I'll give you a piece of good advice: make nice, vague motions for a while, and we'll sort it out for you. But if you start flogging away at us we're screwed." And he's absolutely right.' More laughter.

Previn, who has quit smoking as many times as Mark

Twain, accepted a cigarette from a young man who was sitting in the front row. 'That happened to me once in a piece of Maxwell Davies's,' Previn said. 'I made the mistake of thinking I knew it from memory. One of those pieces where I wanted to send him a congratulatory wire for having two bars in the same metre in a row. I suddenly realised, "God, I don't know what's happening." So I just kind of looked elegant for four bars, and the orchestra fixed it for me. If I'd gone on, wildly beating eleven-sixteenths, we would *never* have got out of the hole. I was very grateful to them.'

A hand went up, and a student asked, 'Was it hard for you to learn technique – beating different time signatures?'

Previn said, 'You can teach anyone technique – how to wave a stick. Of course, since both hands are involved, independence of hand movement – one from the other – is necessary. But the interpretive part – how much you can get out of an orchestra, at what particular time – is hard to learn. Monteux once asked me, "Did you like the way they played the Mozart?" I sensed a trap, but said, "Yes, Maître." He said, "Well, next time, leave them alone." ' Laughter.

Previn said, 'But to get back to your question. When I was a kid, I went to watch a rehearsal. I don't remember who the conductor was, or which orchestra. He was doing a phenomenally complicated piece, the Symphony in C of Stravinsky, which has a movement absolutely *wild* in metric changes. I was sitting there, and I thought, in totally private, serious, honest contemplation, and depression, "I am never *ever* going to be able to do that." It quite threw me. About four years ago, I was doing that piece in London, and a couple of students from the academy came backstage during the break in rehearsal. One of them said, "I'm *so* depressed. That's something I'm never going to learn." The whole thing came flooding back at me, and I was able to say, with complete honesty, "*Sure* you will. This piece did that to me years ago, and it's nothing – no problem at all." But you'll find, with time and experience, that you can't dissociate one from the other – technique and interpretation. I took an orchestra on tour, and discovered the concert would be in a hall so dreadful in every respect that it was insulting to the orchestra. I decided to hell with the community. I'm going to contribute *nothing* to this; I'll just beat time through the Schubert symphony. But two minutes into the symphony I realized I couldn't do that to Schubert, and at the end I felt it was one of the best performances I'd ever conducted of that work. It came closer to living up to the music than my previous attempts at it.'

A hand went up. 'Do you mean *no* performance ever lives up to the music?'

Previn said, 'Sometimes a performance of a second-rate piece can be *better* than the piece. But with a great piece you have to resign yourself to the fact that the music will always be better than any performance. You often hear conductors say, "my Brahms", "my Mozart", "my Beethoven". That's *unforgivable*. When you feel you've matched your interpretation with Schubert's genius, what are you going to shoot for next time? The best you can do is not be ashamed of a performance.'

The same student asked, 'How do you feel about performances of *your* music?'

Previn said, 'This isn't modesty but realism. Of *course* performers can make it as good as it is. Usually better.' He laughed, and added, 'I'm *counting* on Ashkenazy making my piano concerto better than it is.' Laughter.

Previn continued, 'Seriously, I think that when you hear a great performance, if you were to examine it, it's great because it's unlocked audibly some of the genius of the piece the way the composer wrote it. When Perlman plays the Brahms Concerto, Karajan conducts the Mahler nine – there are other examples – the reason you think it's so transcendentally *wonderful* is because it's made you realize how great the *piece* is. The reason Karajan – one of the greatest conductors of the century – closes his eyes when he conducts is because he can commune with the music, without the interruption of seeing an oboe player fix a reed, or whatever. But a conductor is supposed to communicate to the orchestra, which, in turn communicates to the audience. I don't know how Karajan manages, but he does. So he's one up on all of us. From my own point of view, I can convey a lot by looking, and having the musicians look at me. I even feel that with some music you can *look* someone into doing something more than you can gesticulate them into doing it.'

Meier asked him how he approached a new score – how he studied it.

Previn said, 'You see, everyone does it in a different way, so I can't tell you "the right way", in quotes. If it's a score that one can struggle through at the piano, then I will do that. But, obviously, with contemporary scores that's not always possible. I can't take a Xenakis score and get through it on the piano. It can't be done. So then it becomes a matter of application of technique – a previous knowledge of a certain pattern. But if it's a symphony or a standard piece that, by accident, I've not done, it helps me, in general, as a pianist who doesn't mind transpositions, to play through it. Some conductors never make any marks on their scores, and I find that admirable. I mark up my scores to an *insane* degree – with private codes, numbers, whatever, to which I never refer once I know the piece. Nowadays, all of us who have our own orchestras and travel a lot are faced with too much repertoire, and sometimes we're really not given enough time to learn a piece. So any mnemonics can help. I've seen it done with colours, pictures, numbers – anything. I think *everything's* fair. I don't believe in learning a piece off a record, though there are exceptions even to that – if, for instance, there's an emergency and you have to make a change in the programme overnight. A soloist says, "I'm not going to play the Brahms. I'm going to play a piano concerto by Spohr." ' Laughter. 'If it's obviously something that you're not going to ever use again, then if there's a record by all means listen to it, look at the score, get an idea. The other thing is, if there's an extremely complicated piece I do like to hear it once to see what the aural image is. But the problem with learning from records – If you're doing it, there's no harm in it, but I wouldn't recommend it for very long, because you might wind up learning somebody else's performance. I read recently, to my absolute amazement, that one of the world's great conductors said in an interview that he learns *everything* from records. I don't have any criticism of it. I find it extraordinary (a) that he does it, and (b) even more extraordinary that he *admits* it. The interviewer said "Whose?" – which is fair enough – and he said that it had to be someone he genuinely admired. He said he knew that a lot of his colleagues would have disdain for that. He also said, "It works for me, and I find I don't copy someone's performance. I find that it cuts my work load." And he's certainly got it made.'

Previn accepted another cigarette and asked, 'How many of you work from records?'

Most of the hands went up, and one young man volunteered, 'Sometimes I'll listen to six different recordings of a work, almost as a form of research, to get different approaches, hear how different problems are solved – a number of opinions, without focusing on one. An assimilation, perhaps.'

Previn said quickly, 'But that has its *own* trap: you then start figuring which one you like best, you know? Instead of working it out. If you hear a Mahler symphony by Haitink and Bernstein and Kubelik and Levine, you'll have a favourite, and the trouble is that you'll at least subconsciously gravitate toward the one you like the best. On the other hand, it might not do any harm, because when you rehearse a big piece you'll find that imitative things don't come naturally or normally, and if you have that within you which eventually does make the professional conductor, I think, at that *moment*, even if you meant to do – and let's be simplistic – the enormous ritard that Conductor X made on the record, you'll suddenly decide that it's not comfortable for you, and you'll do something else. So perhaps there's no great harm in listening to records while you're learning repertoire. There should be no harangues about it.'

A hand went up. 'You said once you've learned a score you don't look at it again, but you seem to always conduct with a score. Why is that?'

Previn said, 'I like to have a score in front of me onstage. It gives me a sense of security. Concertos are a different matter. In the standard repertoire, if there is something in a particular spot that, say, Isaac Stern wants, I will mark that in the score with his initials, so the next time we do that particular piece no discussion will be necessary.' He paused, and then said, 'You've reminded me of something. Radu Lupu is one of my favourite pianists – a very great artist. We'd toured with the LSO doing the Schumann and Greig concertos. We also recorded them before doing them in a concert in Festival Hall. That music was *ingrained* in both of us, so, although I had the score in front of me, I didn't bother looking at it. In the Grieg he played like an angel, and I knew everything he was going to do. The accompaniment was particularly good. That concerto, as you all know, ends with a series of chords, and suddenly, in my mind – I don't know what possessed me – I thought there was one chord less than there actually is. So after what turned out to be the penultimate chord, I simply stopped conducting. And, instead of one last fortissimo eighth-note chord, WHACK!, from the orchestra, there were about six people, no more, who gave a kind of mouselike mezzo-piano s-k-o-n-k at the end, and Radu looked at me as if he'd been shot. And then he started laughing.' Loud laughter. Previn added, 'Radu has *never* let me up from that.'

Previn asked, 'How many of you can, if not compose, orchestrate? All? Most. Well, that helps. I've seen a lot of young conductors stumped. Every orchestra has a kind of professional conductor-killer. It happens especially with certain of the winds and horns. They'll suddenly stop you and say, "Look, my part's written in E, and I'm playing an A clarinet, and the part's been transposed to B-flat, so is my note a D?" And then when the poor fellow says "Yes", it's *hopeless*. Either you say, "I have no idea what you're talking about", which is perfectly all right, or you really can follow what he's saying – and you can do that more easily if you know scoring. Just blind-faith guessing is wrong.'

Meier asked, 'Is that kind of heckling common?'

'Yes, sure,' Previn said. 'However, I don't think it's just pure bloody-mindedness on the part of the players. I think that an orchestra that faces a number of conductors and puts in a tremendous work load gets bored, and it's in the nature of a game, a form of relaxation. "Let's see if this guy knows anything." Sometimes it's done with more malice and sometimes with less. I don't believe it's ever outright animosity.' Some conductors do provoke animosity in an orchestra. One of the most prominent conductors on the international scene is called the Great Humilitarian; another, pompous and preachy, is called Mighty Mouth; Boulez, who is proud of his sharp ear and is given to having an orchestra tune excessively, is called Charlie the Tuna *and* the French Correction. On the other hand, the Japanese Ozawa is called, with deep affection, the China Doll. 'It could be just a way of relieving the tedium. I have always found it easier to either answer it with a joke – turn it on the player, so *he* looks faintly silly – which the orchestra loves even more or simply say, "I don't know what you're talking about." But to *fall* for it is disastrous. Then you're at a disadvantage forever. It can lead to funny situations. The whole problem of authority with an orchestra is a complex one. And that changes with geography. One of the first times I conducted the Vienna Philharmonic, in the mid-seventies, I was doing the "Linz" Symphony, and I disliked a bowing they were

96

using. I stopped them and said, "Excuse me, but that's an extremely overfussy bowing. Who figured that out for you?" And the concertmaster [leader] said, "Furtwängler".' Previn laughed. 'Well, at that point either you can say "The concert's off", and go home, or you can insist on changing it. And, in a curious way, insisting on changing it – if your suggestion really works – will make bigger points than to give in to a tradition. But if they try yours and then you decide you actually like the first bowing better, you must say so. It's a scary moment when they throw some big name at you. But avoid a complete capitulation. And, by the way, it might not be true. The bowing could have come from a concertmaster who was fired the year before. They just want to check up on you. It's an interesting small war, but it's never really serious. No orchestra is out to get you, because, among other things, once you're up there they know they're stuck with you for a week, or whatever. They always have the out of getting word to the management that they don't want you again. But for that week they're stuck with you. And if they're any kind of orchestra they'll want the concert to be good. They don't *want* you to be bad. So you always have to figure that for now they would like you to be terrific, and it helps to know that. It's extraordinary, in a way. Orchestras don't mind if you're very bad. They don't like to be bored. The worst thing I can remember – again, it was the Vienna. Not too long ago, in Salzburg – a special Sunday-afternoon concert, given by a conductor I didn't know. Local talent. They did "Serenata Notturna", the G-Minor, and the "Jupiter". It was very beautiful. They played *so* wonderfully, the Vienna Philharmonic, with the programme – all that Mozart. The next day, I was rehearsing with the orchestra, and during one of the breaks I said to the concertmaster, "Yesterday, that programme, which was really wonderfully played – what did that conductor, whom you had not worked with before, bring to that concert of himself? What did he add?" And the concertmaster said, "Well, he wore his tails." You

97

might as well jump out the window. If he had said, "He ruined it by being arbitrary and doing things that we hated", that would have been almost a reverse compliment: he was making his presence felt. But they hadn't even known he was there. The whole thing of people saying, "Look out for this orchestra, or that orchestra" – famous stories about the New York Philharmonic, or the Chicago, or the Concertgebouw, or whatever – I've found to be ninety-nine per cent legend. Orchestra players, even under the most adverse conditions, are usually extremely admirable people. There may be four, five, six in every orchestra that cause problems, but that's because they *have* problems, not because they particularly want to make them. I find it very easy to get along with good orchestras. They're all proud of being there. If they don't like you at all, they'll play well to spite you, to show you that it's possible. Generally speaking, orchestra musicians are marvellous.'

A hand went up. 'I'd like to ask you a question about interpretative traditions – particularly present traditions. It seems that in every generation performers bring to their interpretations of older music what's going on at present in their musical lives. Now that one of the most dominant aspects of performance is to clean up the excesses of those nineteenth-century editions, and there's a trend toward a more individual input, I'm wondering if you feel we've arrived at a point where there's no place else to go' – Previn interjected, 'I hope not' – 'or if you feel that the present phenomenon might give way to something else.'

Previn said, 'Well, if it does, it won't be of our volition, because I don't think it's possible to be an artist, whether it's interpretative or creative, and live in a vacuum. I think everything affects us – absolutely everything. The unrest or ease of the world, the weather, our personal lives. And I think that when things change they change so gradually in terms of musical tastes that we're likely not to be terribly aware of it. It's easy now to hear recordings that were made in the late twenties and say "How could anybody play Bach with a piano for continuo, and ten basses in the orchestra?" But those things change almost imperceptibly. Nobody suddenly says, "OK. Now we're going to do such-and-such." I don't think that we have much choice about it. I think everybody in this room would agree that the way people approach Mozart and Haydn and earlier music now is to be preferred to the excesses that were made in the editions of the nineteenth century. But whether a hundred years from now people sitting around in this room would agree with us I don't know. I *like* the fact that music is so unpredictably quixotic – that it reflects the philosophy of everything that goes on in the whole world – and therefore I think that to worry about traditions of the past or possible solutions in the future is fine if you are writing a book, but if you're actually going to get up and do it you have to follow a purely personal conviction.'

A young man said, 'About composers – with the exception of Schönberg and Stravinsky, there are no great composers of this century.'

Koussevitzky, who once warned conductors that if they ignored new works composers could be discouraged from composing and in the future there would be no 'old' music for anyone to conduct, would have applauded Previn's answer. 'But you don't know that. Nor do I. Someone might be writing his tail off right now, and we don't know it.'

The same young man said, 'But Stravinsky was recognised when he was only twenty-six.'

Previn said, 'Yes, and, on the other hand, Tchaikovsky had no use for Brahms, and thought Rubinstein was a better composer. You just don't know. Everybody has perfect hindsight. When you talk about history, you tend to telescope a century. You say, "The nineteenth century was phenomenal because – " and then list everyone in it.

The fact that the composers were geographically separated and decades apart is no longer significant in retrospect. In the twenty-first century, it's very likely someone will say of the twentieth century, "Boy, it was terrific", and start naming everyone who is terrific now. It's going to be a very imposing list. The only thing that's missing now – and this is understandable – is the public supportive enthusiasm. I think the alienation between the composer's output and the public's taste is greater than it's ever been. When Brahms had a new symphony, Puccini a new opera, people looked *forward* to it. They couldn't *wait*. "In six months, we're going to hear it." "In four months." It was a gigantic event. And now – not just among the general public but a public that is concert-minded – how many *know* that there's going to be a new Elliot Carter? Or give a goddam? That's a shame. But it's undeniable.'

A student asked if that was perhaps because the musical language of modern composers was different from the public perception of what that language should be.

Previn said, 'Well, possibly not of what it should be but of what it should be for them. Have any of you read a book by Nicolas Slonimsky, *Lexicon of Musical Invective*?' A laugh here and there indicated that a few had. 'The world's most entertaining reading. It's a collection of excerpts from reviews. You'll read something like "Well, I heard a piece last night, and unfortunately it doesn't have a tune in it, and it will never be played again", and it's Brahms One. And you think, "How can they *say* that? Doesn't have a tune in it!" So there's always been resistance to new music. But not as much as now. Because today the kind of event where a new work is played, and played around the world, is very rare – truly, truly rare. And it is because the vocabulary has got, if you like, so sophisticated – or, if you're on the other side of the fence, so needlessly complicated – that it alienates people at the first hearing. What I'm convinced of, though, is that familiarity breeds liking. That may sound like a paradox, but it's true, and if one heard a brand-new piece by a new composer with the

100

deadening regularity that we hear Tchaikovsky Five a lot more people would love it. And it's entirely possible that some extremely angular line would become as familiar to our ear as the most diatonic theme in the world.'

A student said, 'But there are certain criteria not met by most modern composers. People want to hear something melodic, with a certain structure.'

Previn said, 'But "melodic" is an absolutely personal thing. If I had to give you a music-dictionary definition of "melodic", it would be difficult. A melody is really just a succession of notes. I suspect you're saying that people like music to be relaxing, passive listening. Most audiences sit at a concert the way you sit in a warm bath. It's extremely pleasant. I'm glad they've come. But it's a passive experience, not an active one. If you *make* them listen, *make* them participate, they often grow tired very quickly. Aaron Copland said that listening is a talent that can be developed, like playing. And that's why the playing of new music is so necessary. And you'll find, as your careers develop, that it is not just audiences that resist new music but orchestras, too. They do *not* want to play it. It's damned hard work. Very often, they struggle through this complex mass and they don't get a sense of the whole. All they know is, it's very hard – too many string crossings, difficult horn parts – and they don't want to know more. They'd much rather spend their time playing more familiar and, hence, "easier" music. It's a kind of cabal. Conductors don't particularly want to go through the agony of figuring a piece out; orchestras don't want to go through the agony of rehearsing it; and the audience doesn't want to hear it. It's three strikes in a row, and you have to fight that. I'm not one of those people who are messianic about it – I take no credit for that. I don't programme music because it's new. I programme it because it *says* something to me. I did Messiaen's "Turangalila" Symphony with the Chicago Symphony – three performances. I had to fight about two-thirds of that orchestra at every rehearsal. They would come up at the break complaining, "This is *killing*", and "Are you kidding?" In that case, it was music I felt strongly about, and I had all kinds of answers.' Previn did the Messiaen in Pittsburgh, too – also three performances. The first night, a lot of people walked out. The next night, he made a speech before he began, explaining something about the music and asking the audience to give it a chance. The reception was better, and after the third performance, a Sunday-afternoon concert, he got what he called 'a *crouching ovation*'. Previn continued, 'There are American composers, like George Rochberg, who have written a little bit of everything and are very popular. Some young composers have concentrated almost exclusively on writing for small groups, thus making sure they will get to hear their music. Naturally, it's easier to get five or ten people together than an entire orchestra. But some current composers have been re-seduced by the orchestra; I'm in the happy position of knowing, because so many scores are submitted to me.'

Meier asked Previn to tell the students something about the social demands made on a conductor.

Previn said, 'Some people feel that a concert is a necessary prelude to the party. I disapprove of that so *violently* that I suppose I've made a lot of enemies by simply not going along with it. I feel that what the conductor owes the city is to work like crazy until the last cutoff – the final note. After that, you don't owe people *anything* until the next rehearsal. Because either they feel that the music, the orchestra, the community interest in music have been worth the work expended or they don't. I don't want someone to give the orchestra an extra fifty thousand dollars just because I've played tennis with him. That is, if you like, unrealistic. A lot of conductors are very good at socialising. I'm not – I'm not used to it. And, of course, I've never been music director of a community orchestra. Fund-raising is necessary, it exists, it has to be faced, but I've been luxuriating in the fact that I don't have to do it.'

Miss Deutsch asked, 'Doesn't the Pittsburgh board give you a hard time?'

Previn said, 'No, they don't. Again, I'm very lucky. I've quite on purpose – this sounds self-aggrandising, and I don't mean it that way – got across the fact that I'm an eccentric who won't come to parties. They've given up on me, and that's fine. The day they decide I'm doing a bad job with the orchestra, they'll fire me, which is their prerogative. Until then, I don't have to worry about the social end of it.

'In London, the situation doesn't exist. In London, two very odd things exist: there aren't many subscriptions. Most concerts start with the sale of Ticket One. Can you imagine how difficult that makes programme planning? In the States, because of the subscription system, you can have much more freedom in planning – the luxury of putting on new works. And by new I don't necessarily mean the latest work. I mean unfamiliar. People may elect not to come, and therefore, with an adventurous pro-gramme, you'll have an empty house. But empty house or not, the seat has been paid for, so that the major economic struggle has already been decided. In London, if you put on something that is not to the public's taste, you're *really* in trouble, because people won't buy the ticket to begin with. That's number one. Number two, of course, is that the four big London orchestras are self-governing. The management is the employee of the orchestra. The orchestra can fire the manager, fire the conductor, fire anybody. They run it. There is also a third point. Orchestras are partly government-subsidised, so once a year we go to the Arts Council of Great Britain and do our beggar's act.'

Previn paused a second, and then laughed. 'When I first came to Pittsburgh after those years in London, I had a meeting with the orchestra committee. After we'd dis-cussed a few things, I said, "Well, gentlemen, what would

103

you like to play in the coming year?" Sy Rosen, who was the managing director then, said, "Could I talk to you for a minute?" He took me outside and said, "Don't ask them that." And I said, "But they're the ones who'll have to play it." He mumbled, "Yes, but don't do that – don't ask them." ' Previn tells a good story, and there was an explosion of laughter. 'About half an hour later, after we'd covered some agenda, I said, "Well, gentlemen, would you like to tour next year?" and Sy said, "Can I see you for a minute?" ' Enormous laughter. 'Now, years later, I've tried to get it somewhere in the middle. Because it's certainly true that, with the situation that exists here, management must make the decisions. The ripples widen. The management goes to the board. The board gets the money. The money pays for the tours, et cetera. But at the same time what I've *tried* to convey – and I'm only partly successful – is that I think that the players, even if they can't change anything, ought to be *in* on it, so that you don't say to them, "This season, we're going to the Orient for six weeks." They ought to know that two years before, when it's first planned, so that they can either look forward to it, or dread it, or quit, or something. If I say, "We're going to commission five pieces next year by the following people", a step better would be for me to say, "We're going to commission five pieces next year. I have several people in mind. If you have any suggestions, let me hear them." It's my prerogative to turn them down, but I think players are much too valuable to be treated as if they were mindless. Critics, when they want to be kind, say that the orchestra is the conductor's instrument. I find that very offensive, because the orchestra is *not* an instrument. It's not made of inanimate objects. It's made up of all those people with a lifetime of practising, ambitions realised and unrealised, other disappointments.' The students applauded, and so did Meier.

A hand went up. 'Tell us something about programming.'

Previn said, 'Again, it depends very much on geography. In England, since there are few subscriptions, programmes are designed to make sense between eight and ten, just for that one evening. That's what audiences like. But here, where programmes are planned at least a year in advance, you can try for a season that has some kind of profile. You can say, "I'd like to do a Sibelius cycle", or "I'll do American music of the turn of the century up to the thirties." I'm fabricating wildly, of course. "I want to do post-Ravel French music." And you can slot it in during the season. And because *that* makes sense, sometimes the works *around* those works can be seemingly quite crazy. But they'll make horizontal sense, if not vertical sense. In Europe, we have to make every programme make sense within itself. It's a different set of problems. I, personally, am not terribly in favour of all-anything programmes, unless it's Mozart. Some people do all-Brahms, all-Tchaikovsky, all-Prokofiev programmes – I'm not sure it's terribly interesting. Unless, of course, it's an anniversary. All-Mozart programmes are nice, and always surprising. I find Mozart will say anything to you that you think he's saying. If you find that the G-Minor Symphony is an expression of enormous virility, there it is. Or an expression of immense angst. It will mirror back anything you bring to it. And that's not the case with most composers.'

One young man said he was interested in the order in which to present a given programme. He said he conducted a civic orchestra.

Previn said, '*Don't* put the new work last. The audience will leave.' He continued, 'I don't think it's necessary to go by historical chronology. It's good to go by the sort of sound that will assault the ear. If you particularly want to do a "Daphnis", or one of the big, big Strauss pieces, or, let's say, a Respighi piece, it's *got* to be last, because the ear is *tired*. You can't follow that with anything – it's impossible. On the other hand, the fact that the time-honoured thing is to start with a "courtesy" piece for those people who will be late I resent *bitterly*.' Laughter. 'You can work out a very nice programme: a major Haydn, a minor symphony, the interval, and then whatever, and the manager says to you, "We really ought to have a five-minute overture. Anything will do." And that's because a lot of people haven't found the evening valid enough to come on time. I *really* resent that. I don't like courtesy pieces. I call them parking-lot overtures.' The student conductors laughed. 'Other than that, all of you, when you begin to do a lot of concerts you're going to encounter a lot of problems that are, if you like, extramusical. If you have a very great soloist, he's probably going to want to play after the interval. And he's got a right. That's fine. So then you have to adjust. Maybe even reprogramme things. Again, certain pieces are not actually long but do too much to you to be followed by anything. A *terrible* habit in England is the feeling that a programme should be eighty minutes long, give or take a minute. So that if a piece is seventy minutes long they want an additional ten-minute piece. And what that does to programming is unspeakable. Sometimes, in the States, programmes tend to be shorter than that, and I'm all in favour of it – and not for reasons of personal tiredness. I just think that a certain amount of great music is enough. When people ask me how long a particular piece is, I don't know. I'm no good at that. I know when a piece seems long and when it seems short. Once, I was backstage in Festival Hall, and Isaac Stern was the soloist. He was to play the Sibelius, which the BBC would broadcast. A fellow from the station came up to us and asked Isaac, "How long is the Sibelius?" Isaac said he didn't know, and I said, "It's twenty-nine minutes." The man left, and Isaac said, "Is it really that long?" I said, "I have no idea." But I made the fellow happy, and if it had run thirty-one he would have taken it as an aberration of the evening. He wanted a figure, and I wanted him off my hands. Some people are remarkable at timing. I know a manager – I don't know where he is now. He was ubiquitous. A walking encyclopedia of timing. He used to say to me, "Such-and-such is terrific. It's twelve and a half minutes." And I never knew if he thought the piece was terrific in and of itself or because it was twelve and a half minutes. He was infallible. Amazing. But to continue about programming – there are a lot of problems involved. I think that if some connection can be made, or some contrast that makes sense, it's something to keep in mind. Certain juxtapositions you just can't do. But some you can. Once, I did the "Wozzeck" excerpts just before the interval. After the interval, the same singer did the Samuel Barber "Knoxville", written much later. And all of a sudden we were back in diatonic country. It was very interesting. Both written on very valid texts, with one composer extremely conservative. Even if the point was private, it was worth making.'

A hand went up. 'There was a strong nationalistic trend at one time, and I'd like to know if you think the Vienna Philharmonic has the inside track, an innate understanding, when it comes to Schubert, and whether the English musicians have a better understanding, a more legitimate style, when it comes to Vaughan Williams, and also whether you think the English audiences themselves are more open to Vaughan Williams than to a German or Viennese or Italian composer.'

Previn said, 'That's an interesting question. Get me back on the track if I go too far afield. Certain orchestras have the inside track not because they necessarily have an instinct for certain music but because they have the *history* of the music. The Vienna Philharmonic has probably played Schubert more consistently and more often than any other orchestra, and therefore there's a kind of in-built tradition. The ease, the familiarity, is not just within one player but within his father and his grandfather as well, and that leaves a mark. It does not mean that another musician does not play the music as well. It's just *easier* for the Vienna to associate themselves mentally with

107

that music. To be the devil's advocate – there are things that are extremely nationalistic in music, and I like that. Just think about the prevalence of folk influence on music and you'll realise – though music is much more international now – that nationalism exists. If you do "American in Paris" with the Chicago Symphony – never mind the fact that they *know* it. Let's say that they're sight-reading. They would know what to do because it is not possible to grow up in this country without hearing offshoots of that kind of music. I'm not proposing that that piece has anything to do with jazz, though it certainly is peripherally in that mould. That kind of syncopation, that kind of melody, is on the radio. Whether they want to hear it or not, they grew up with it. So the Chicago musicians are going to know instinctively how to phrase that music – much more than, say, the Royal Danish. Conversely – never mind Schubert – when the Vienna Philharmonic plays a Strauss waltz –' He broke off and asked, 'How many of you have ever conducted a Strauss waltz?'

Every hand shot up.

Previn said, 'OK. Is there anything in the world that is harder to rehearse? I find it *killing*. It's *really* hard to get that unspoken lilt – never mind the fact that the second beat is anticipated. I've heard the greatest orchestras in the world attempt that, and even when they do it well it's not natural, it's not absolutely perfect. The Vienna Philharmonic presses the "Blue Danube" button, and off the players go, and it's perfect. You can either listen to it or dance to it – or whatever. *I* don't know how they do that. It's just that, even if they haven't played it, they've grown up hearing it all their lives. By the same token, Copland's music is much easier to rehearse in this country. That kind of jaggedness, which is extremely American – even if musicians here haven't played a particular Copland piece before, it's in their subconscious. That much is true. But if they try to tell you in Berlin that they are the only ones who know how to play Brahms, for instance, which is a popular conceit on their part – no. That's nonsense. But if

108

things are based on a nationalistic, folkloric tradition, then it's true.'

Previn accepted another cigarette, and said, 'There was a second part to your question. There was another facet.'

'It was about the receptiveness of the audiences themselves.'

Previn said, 'At one time, it is true, music was a lot less exportable. There was a great deal of chauvinism about nationalistic music, and in England they tended not to send out Elgar, Vaughan Williams. The only thing they sent out was Delius, which was never very English to begin with. I mean, he lived in France and Florida.' Laughter. 'And here. We didn't tend to send out William Schuman's pieces, or even Copland's. In the last quarter of the century, with the diminishing of the size of the world in every aspect, that breach has been closed. You'll now find a very enthusiastic reception for an Elgar symphony in Germany, and you'll find a great reception for Henze in the United States.'

Miss Deutsch interrupted. 'Rachmaninoff. He's *so* familiar here. *We* accept the fact that he's a great composer. Is it the same in Europe?'

Previn said, 'That's interesting. I've always felt that there's a reticence in *this* country about Rachmaninoff, because while people all think it's extremely *pretty* they're ashamed to *like* it. They'll say, "Well, of course it's wonderful, but it's not *serious*." At least, our learned pressmen think that. In Europe, he's taken seriously. Not in Germany. Not in Austria. I have to say that to you. I once proposed doing the Rachmaninoff Second in Salzburg, and they looked at me as if I'd suggested Marvin Hamlisch.' Boisterous laughter. When the laughter stopped, he said, 'But then in Germany I did the *Peter Grimes* excerpts, and the next day the critics said I did the music from "the film *Peter Grimes*". But Rachmaninoff is taken seriously elsewhere in Europe, and by now nobody even makes cuts. The Second Symphony takes its sixty-minute toll, and that's it. I find there's always that niggling thing in the States, though. People like it, are enthusiastic about it, and vaguely embarrassed. It's curious. To finish it off: in 1971, I took the LSO to Russia, and we did the Rach Second and the "Symphonic Dances" – five programmes. They had been heard so seldom, if *ever* – and I cannot *tell* you what happened. Russian audiences tend to be emotional anyway. People wept openly. The music really said something to them, for whatever reasons – emotional or political or both.' Rachmaninoff left Russia in 1917, and died in Los Angeles twenty-six years later. Previn continued, 'Again, it's an extremely nationalistic sound, unmistakably Slavic, and it reached them and grabbed them by the throat. Possibly it was coincidence, but after we left they began playing the Second and the "Dances" there, and recording them. A couple of years later, when I went back as a guest conductor in Leningrad, they wanted the Third Symphony and "The Isle of the Dead." '

Miss Deutsch changed the subject. She asked how one went about getting a manager.

Previn, without naming his own manager, Ronald Wilford, said he'd just lucked out, and then asked, 'Why don't you, or somebody, tell me about your experiences? Seriously – about finding a manager, not finding one, being turned down.'

One student said, 'I was in Germany, and I was told I needed more experience, so I came to the United States, where I was told I needed more experience, and I returned to Germany. I've made that back-and-forth trip three times, and I've made more contacts, but I was told in no uncertain terms that I couldn't get anywhere without experience. Give up everything in Germany and move here. Or don't come back here until I've at least conducted the Berlin Philharmonic.'

Previn asked the students if this experience was typical,

and all hands went up. He said, 'That surprises me, because Mr Meier, here, told me last night that there are twenty-six hundred orchestras in the United States.'

Meier said, 'Of course, that includes orchestras that have one concert a year.'

Previn said, 'When you go to a manager with the express wish that he either advise you or represent you, what do you take to him? Your clippings, or tapes, or recommendations?'

Mr Ling said, 'I think I can speak for everyone here. Résumé, photographs, reviews of concerts, recommendations, a list of repertoire, performances.'

Previn said, 'The only two things that would interest me are repertoire lists and recommendations. Reviews are not always particularly interesting, and, to be blunt, when you're beginning a career, where are you likely to *get* reviews? In places that would simply not interest a New York manager. You were absolutely brilliant in Ames, Iowa. So what? On those occasions when I've had the luxury of trying to find an assistant, in London or in Pittsburgh, and people bring me *sheets* of reviews, certainly I read them, but they don't mean much to me. But when the candidate says, "I know such-and-such repertoire", I would rather that he'd done that repertoire with an amateur orchestra that nobody was listening to than he'd given a performance of Beethoven One someplace that someone on a newspaper liked. Also, it carries a lot of weight with me when a colleague of mine recommends someone, and I can't see that it wouldn't carry a lot of weight with a manager.'

Meier said to Previn, 'What criteria do *you* follow? If a manager comes to you and says, "I've got this wonderful conductor who conducts the symphony in Poughkeepsie and he has a marvellous repertoire", I don't think you would buy it. If he says instead, "He has the recommendation of Abbado", that conductor would have more of a chance. Am I right?'

Previn said, 'Yes, and I'll tell you something else. Those

of us who conduct tend to be in one place a lot of the time. Soloists travel much more than conductors do, and the biggest soloists in the world play in a lot of tiny cities in between big dates, as you well know. Whenever I have a big soloist – Zukerman, Perlman, Ashkenazy, Stern – I always say, "Where have you just come from?" and they often name some surprisingly small city, and I ask "How was it – how was the conductor?" If one of them says, "You know, he was damned good", I will remember that, and possibly use him in the future. So if you can get a soloist to put in a good word for you that can help a lot. Soloists travel more, and they know more than managers or conductors.' He paused. 'This must all sound very lame. I just don't know what the answer is.'

Meier said, 'What about the coat-tail theory – the takeover? Like Tilson Thomas for William Steinberg; Bernstein for Bruno Walter. Isn't it more recommendable to be an *assistant* to a big shot than to have your own orchestra on a third level?'

Previn said, 'Absolutely. Colin Davis, in England, was given very short notice to jump in for someone, and he managed it. That started things. He'll be here next week. You can ask him. I think if you have a chance to be in *any* position, no matter how seemingly menial it is, with a good orchestra – be around it, live that life, see what it entails, do the children's concert, or whatever – then you *will* have the chance to do that subscription series eventually, either by design or by accident. And that's a lot better than being Number One someplace where the world's music is never made. The dependence on managers is one of those imponderables. Last night, when I arrived to do the concert, I was handed a very long telegram about a young pianist. It was from a manager. In the last sentence, he said, "Ask Mr Ozawa about her." And I did, and Seiji said she was sensational. I'll make a point of hearing her. Seiji *can't* be wrong when he's that enthusiastic about someone. And the same would apply to a young conductor. So a manager or a conductor would

112

pay more attention to a recommendation than to any number of résumés.'

Meier said, 'I hope you have a lot of stationery with you.' An explosion of laughter, and one of the students, through the laughter, said, 'Just *sign* it. We'll do the rest.'

Previn said, 'Unfortunately, it's necessary to *see* someone in action. A lot of people talk a terrific Brahms symphony.' The laughter subsided, and Previn went on, 'I always feel, in a curious way, guilty when I have the pleasure of talking to a roomful of young people who want to conduct, because of that old saw "It's the only thing you can't practise at home." I'm aware of that, and I don't know what the solution is. I was lucky enough to be given the chance to go around and conduct terrible orchestras. And even *that* opportunity was hard to get. There is no answer.' He looked depressed.

Meier said, 'I have an answer. In Europe – Munich, Zurich, and so on – very fine orchestras have subscription series: a top series, with famous conductors and soloists. People will pay a hundred francs, or whatever, and it's sold out. Then they have a second series for the lesser known, and even a third series with completely unknown conductors. It becomes organic.' Previn interrupted, 'That's *wonderful*.' Meier continued, 'Why is it not possible that the Pittsburgh Symphony have a series of four or five concerts with unknown people? Would that not go over?'

Previn said, 'Yes, I think it would – with the audience. I might get a kickback from the orchestra. But it's certainly a valid idea.'

Meier said, 'There's another problem in the United States. You have fine conductors with community orchestras, and they know the repertory, but if you put them someday with the New York Philharmonic they will pee in their pants. What can you say to the New York Philharmonic after conducting a community orchestra? It's like driving a truck all your life and then being given a Mercedes. You'd go off the road.'

Previn said, 'What you say is true. We had auditions in

London a couple of years ago, and a lot of people applied. We made the orchestra available for three days and we just sat and listened to all these people conduct. There was a young man from up north – Middlesborough. He conducted the first movement of the Beethoven Seventh – from beginning to end, without stopping. When it was over, he said, "Thank you very much", and walked off. I ran after him and said, "Listen, you've got all the time in the world. Don't you want to do something? I mean, was that *it* for you?" He was very dear, and what he said was something that I understand. "You know, I have only conducted student orchestras, and I live in a place that is not geographically near a city where great orchestras play, and, except for records, I've never even *heard* one. What I just heard in a run-through was so infinitely better than anything I've ever been able to imagine that I haven't got the guts to tell them anything." ' Sympathetic laughter. 'That's all very lovable, but it's also the end of the road for him. I was sorry I couldn't help him. I had to consider the orchestra. They're sitting there. They don't particularly *want* to play Beethoven's Seventh at that given moment, and here's a fellow who conducts them through it, and they're playing on automatic pilot, and when it's over, he walks off. What's he proven to them?'

Meier, who is tenacious in his desire to help young conductors, asked, 'How did you pick your assistant?'

Previn said, 'I had my choice of three people. The board said, "You can devise your own system for auditioning." I found out that over that season we had three what I think are called county concerts in various universities, usually with repertoire that had been covered that season. Nothing extremely daunting. I had the three do a concert each, and the choice was crystal clear to me. But I had the orchestra vote on the three, and their choice was mine.'

Meier asked, 'How did you pick the three?' Laughter.

Previn laughed, too, and said, 'I didn't pick them. Somehow I arrived at them through the system. The concerts themselves were almost meaningless – but not to

114

the three, of course. I wanted to find out how the orchestra felt – what the sixteenth violinist had to say about them. I wanted the orchestra to like the choice. It took some doing, but I did find a very good person.'

Previn paused for a second, and then said, 'I'm sure none of you will agree with this, because you've reached this level – Tanglewood – but very often I've talked with budding conductors, and I'll say "What are you going to do next season?," and very often they'll say, "I've been offered a job conducting the road company of some musical", and they'll add, "But, of course, I'm not going to do that", and I'll say, "Why not?" I don't understand. I really don't. Orchestral experience, to me, is not necessarily conducting "Ein Heldenleben". Orchestral experience is any situation, in any venue, where you are faced with living people playing instruments. If someone says to you, "I'm sorry you can't conduct the New Jersey Symphony, but would you like to conduct the Ice Capades?" – *do* it!'

Bursts of laughter. And one student said, 'You can say that because you're the exception to the rule.'

Over the laughter, Previn said, 'Well, that's because I've had such a crummy past.' Laughter. 'I spent fifteen years doing films, which is too long. But during that time I faced good players on the average of twice to four times a week with new music. Now, the music may have been from tenth-rate all the way up to third-rate, but so what? It was music that had to be sight-read, cleaned up, and recorded – bang! Like that!' He clapped his hands. 'In as short a time as possible. The players were good, and I think that what I learned in 1950 about getting a score for an animated cartoon straightened out still worked for me when I rehearsed the Vaughan Williams here. You see, if a good player in a symphony orchestra has it in his background to have played in a pit somewhere, no one lifts an eyebrow. But any one of us – well, yes, we spent a year conducting *Hello, Dolly!* and they won't have anything to do with us.' He paused and then asked, 'But aren't those barriers being broken down at all?'

115

Someone said, 'We wouldn't know.'

Previn went on, 'Because all those instrumentalists have an opportunity to play. And sometimes that kind of music is our only opportunity to conduct.'

Miss Deutsch said, 'What I find frustrating is when there's a conducting assistantship open and you apply, only three will be heard. For a violin opening, seventy-five applicants will be heard.'

Previn said, 'Again, I have to play the devil's advocate. For a violin audition, a fellow or a woman comes out and plays. But for a conducting audition you have to impress, in the eighteenth-century meaning of that word' – he laughed – 'a whole *orchestra* to be there, *and* pay them to play all day. It's an impracticability. It could be done only if there were a funding programme munificent enough to pay for it.

'One thing I did want to say to you. Again, just from personal experience. God knows, all these things you should disagree with if you feel like it. All of you come from certain instruments. It's a great mistake to let the instrument go, because, you see, as you work more and more there's a *huge, yawning* trap in front of you if you stand on the rostrum day after week after month after year *telling* people how to play, without remembering how *bloody* hard it is. And I think any opportunity you have to physically produce an acceptable sound – I don't care whether it's chamber music, whether it's in public, whether it's for fun, under the most glorified conditions or the most awful ones – *do* it. For myself, I play endless chamber music and quite a few concerti with orchestras. I know from experience that the orchestras I've been most closely associated with *like* the fact that I will take the same specific gamble that they do. In other words, a clarinet player comes in wrong and everyone hears it. But all of us – we give a wrong cue, and it's an inaudible mistake. It's a visual one, but people in the audience don't know. The orchestra will smile happily.' Laughter. 'But if you actually tell them in deed, not in word, that you realise how

116

damned hard it is to play, and you gamble your reputation on a memory slip, on a finger slip, on lack of preparation, on the vagaries of the moment, it's a very good thing. I strongly urge you to keep up with the instrument. It will enable you to give a specific technical instruction that you would otherwise not be able to do.'

If planes and trains, subways and buses adhered to a schedule the way musicians do, life would be more peaceful. Promptly at four, Meier looked at his watch and told the class, 'Tomorrow we meet at the Shed.'

The students applauded, and Previn said, 'You've been very sweet. But you've asked me too many questions about me. I'd like to hear more about you. We're all colleagues, and we're all in the same fraternity. Maybe we can get to some specifics tomorrow. It's very easy for these seminars to turn into a litany of complaints, but maybe I can think of a way to help.' Loud applause.

CHAPTER 3

On Friday morning, I walked around Stockbridge with Previn, who was on his way to a book shop to buy something to read on the trip back to London. He was leaving the next morning. Walking up the street, he talked about the Boston, and Joseph Silverstein. Previn said. 'He is the world's greatest concertmaster. That's not an opinion, that's a fact, like, "Look! It's summer!" ' Suddenly, Previn broke off and crossed the street. He had, out of the corner of his eye, spotted two boys playing tennis. One of them had lobbed the ball over the fence. Previn retrieved the ball and tossed it back. One of the boys said, 'Thank you, Mr Previn.' Previn returned, and continued where he left off. 'There was some raggedness in the strings during the Haydn rehearsal. A kind of rocking. Joey nodded at me, an indication that it was nothing to stop and correct – just exhaustion and the heat.'

Lorin Maazel was leaving the Cleveland Orchestra, and there were rumours that Previn might succeed him. I asked if there was any truth to the rumours, and he said, 'There are only a certain number of conductors with the right repertoire and experience, and I'm sure my name came up, but no, I haven't been asked. If I were offered it, I honestly think I would decline. You see, I'm just crazy about the Pittsburgh. It is very nearly a truly great orchestra. I get so much pleasure from it; I think I would rather make the Pittsburgh great than maintain a Rolls Royce.'

A woman blocked our path. 'Are you who I think you are?' she said.

Previn smiled and said, 'I don't know. Who do you think I am?'

She said, 'I heard the Saturday-night concert. It was

wonderful.' She produced a programme from her handbag and asked for his autograph. A few paces up the street, a man flew out of a shop. He said, 'I heard one of your records last night – your tribute to Art Tatum. Now here you are!'

Previn nodded and smiled, and as we continued walking he said, 'It amazes me. Those records go back twenty-five years. And the films are still pursuing me. Some young orchestra player will come up and say, "I saw a movie on the late-late show. That Previn who did the music – was that your father?" I stroke my beard and say, "No, that was me." ' He was silent for a moment, and then said, 'Everything in this world is point of view, as far as I'm concerned. There's a quite renowned film composer – a *very* nice man. I won't name him. A director whom I like and admire, Norman Jewison, brought this composer to a concert of mine in London some years ago. I conducted the LSO, at the Festival Hall. The Beethoven Ninth. Happily, it was a good performance – very enthusiastically received. Audiences in England are sensational anyway, and there was a great deal of screaming, and all that. The next day, Norman rang me, and he was laughing. He said, "I have to tell you a good story. I had dinner with our composer friend after the concert, and over drinks I said, 'It's nice, isn't it, to see André up there – Festival Hall, London Symphony, Beethoven Ninth, great success, and all that', and our film-composer friend said, 'Certainly, it's fine. But what amazes *me* is how that man blew his career.' " '

We came to a book shop, and inside, after a quick perusal, Previn bought *Joshua Then and Now*, by Mordecai Richler, whose other books he liked, and the new Peter De Vries.

At two on Friday afternoon, Previn rehearsed the Mozart piano quartet with Silverstein, the cellist Jules Eskin, and the violist Burton Fine in the Shed. It was their second, and final, rehearsal. The first one had amused Previn. He told me, 'I was prepared to really dig in, but we just played through it, and then Joey said, "Now let's tell jokes." Well, they work so hard up here, and they're so good. . .'

On Friday afternoon, when they'd finished the first movement, Previn turned his part back to page one, in anticipation of working out certain spots, but the others seemed eager to get on with it. When they had finished the last movement, Previn went backstage with Silverstein, and while Silverstein was wiping the rosin off his violin and carefully tucking it into its case they discussed what they might play next summer. Silverstein said, 'How about one of the Brahms trios?' and Previn said fine, he liked all of them. Maybe the B-Major. Silverstein nodded.

Previn said, 'I'll see you tonight', and went out to the green benches along the left side of the Shed, where the conducting class, with Meier, was waiting to talk to him. Previn sat next to Meier, on a bench that had been turned around to face the others. Some students were sitting on the grass, to be closer. A lawnmower beyond the Shed was gradually wending its way toward the benches.

Previn said, 'I'll tell you something interesting that happened last night, and it was a *direct* result of what you had told me. The manager of the Pittsburgh Symphony was visiting yesterday, just for twenty-four hours, to go over some things. For the next three years, we're going to have a three-week extension of the season – not part of the subscription, and in the nature of a festival. Obviously, in order to make an impact, the first time it will be all Beethoven, which always manages to sell tickets, even in June in a big city. The obvious choice of conductors – Beethoven specialists – were unavailable, and I'm un-available, because I'll be in Salzburg next year during that period of time. So I said to the manager, "How would it be if, during those weeks, since we can't get the greatest Beethoven conductors in the world, if, instead of settling for Rank B, we hire absolutely new conductors that

120

Previn at the piano: he is a composer as well as performer in his own
right of both classical and jazz music.

In the recording studio
(*above*) With his lifelong friend Vladimir Ashkenazy; (*below* and *inset*)
with Sir William Walton. A staunch admirer of his, Previn is also one of
the world's great interpreters of English music.

With Oscar Peterson, an oldtime associate from the fifties, Previn's
golden jazz period.

(*above*) With Ernest Fleischmann who, as managing director of the London Symphony Orchestra at the time, gave Previn his big break when he agreed to the recording session in 1965 which eventually led to the offer of tenure; (*below*) with the LSO. Previn lasted an unprecedented eleven and a half years as principal conductor to this independent, self-governed orchestra.

The multi-faceted Previn
(*above*) On the Morecambe and Wise Show, displaying his considerable talents as TV personality; and (*below*), on a more serious note, in earnest consultation with Peter Pears, Benjamin Britten and Elisabeth Söderstrom.

Previn and the Pittsburgh
(*above*) With one of his favourite pianists, the Cuban-born Horacio Gutiérrez; and (*below*) rehearsing with soloist Eunice Lee.

(*above*) With Michael Lankester, his assistant conductor, on tour in Hong Kong with the Pittsburgh Symphony Orchestra, winter 1984; (*below*) with Carlo Maria Giulini, his predecessor as music director of the Los Angeles Philharmonic.

With his third wife, Heather Hales
(*above*) Against the backdrop of their Surrey home; (*below right*) with
their son Lukas.

nobody ever heard of?" And he said, "Well, I'll have to check with the board on that." ' Laughter. 'I said, "You know, I just went through a whole afternoon of this. *Why* would you?" He said it was a new venture, and he would have to justify it. So, in September, when the season starts, I'll speak to the board and I'll make a pitch. I, frankly, think it would be terrific. I think they could even get a lot of mileage out of the fact that it would be all new conductors, young conductors. I'm grateful to you for giving me that idea. You presented quite a case. The thing that I remembered most is that one of you told me that managers said "Get some orchestral experience" and you said, "That's what I'm dying to have" and they said, "Well, fine. Go and get some." It is truly Joseph Heller. It is unbelievable.'

Previn accepted a cigarette from a young man sitting on the grass, and said, 'Today, some of you wanted to talk about more technical things. Our time is fairly limited. Is there anything you want to tell me, or ask, or discuss?'

A student said, 'To tell you the truth, we'd like to conduct for you.'

Previn said, 'I know, I'd like that. But because of the rehearsal that wasn't possible. We have just thirty minutes. It would be like a conducting competition: "In twenty minutes, do 'The Rite of Spring' and Beethoven's Ninth." ' Everyone laughed.

A student said, 'To us, watching you conduct, it seems you have a very distinctive technical style. Is that something that evolved naturally, as your means of expressing your musical concepts, or did you develop that from seeing people whose technique you admired?'

Previn said, 'Luckily, I don't know what it looks like. I can't watch myself, and I don't watch the television shows. It just evolved, and I have found out – it takes years and years – that it doesn't require an enormous, wide range of physical gestures to get what you want. When I first started, I was criticised for leaping all over the place. Now, very often, when it's an adverse review, they

121

say I *underconduct*. And it's not on purpose – in order to minimise what was wrong in the beginning. Over the years, it wound up whatever I do – good, bad, or indifferent – is the way I work the best. Most of the time, what I'm after seems to be quite clear to people. I don't know what my way of conducting will be like twenty years from now – if I'm still living – but it won't be anything deliberate. In what respect is it different from other people's? Less? More? What?'

One student said, 'It's very yourself', and another said, 'The basic geography, the focus.' Conductors without orchestras can get hung up on technique.

Previn said, 'I feel if you can conduct the phrase, and not the beat, you're very far ahead. If you're going to do "The Rite of Spring", forget it. Conduct the beat.' Laughter. 'If you're doing, say, Strauss or Mahler, or the Romantic repertoire, or even earlier than that, very often you can remind the orchestra of where the phrase is without actually beating the time. Sometimes that puts you in a dangerous corner, but you can feel it coming. Then you can go back to conducting the beat for a little while in an unmistakable metronomic manner – but not for very long. It would make for a not very interesting performance.'

Miss Deutsch asked, 'Did you study gestures?'

'No, no, no. You mean in front of a mirror?'

'Well, Bernstein told us he'd never practised a gesture in his life.'

Previn said, 'Monteux gave me some good advice a long time ago. He saw me do the "Tragic" Overture. Afterward, he said, "Listen, before you knock out the ladies in the balcony make sure the horns come in." Not bad.' Surprised laughter. 'No. I think *anything* you do – any gesture, any exhorting, any cajoling – to get from the orchestra that which you want is OK. Because it is, after all – in the privacy of this meeting – a selfish profession.' He added, 'Not really – not philosophically. It's just that you have to elicit that which you want at the moment.

Anything you do to get that is fair. Whether it's awkward-looking, against the "rules", or whatever, doesn't make any difference. If it provokes the kind of playing you want, *do* it! You have to find out what is your own nature physically. Some people are shy about conducting and turn into wonderful conductors. Some people are extraordinarily extroverted and *that* works. Some people say Bernstein jumps around too much. Nonsense. He gets fabulous performances. Other people say Böhm didn't move at all – nothing happened. It didn't make any difference. It worked for him.'

A student asked Previn to tell them something about playing Mozart concertos with an orchestra and conducting from the keyboard, and also asked whether he did any other composers in this manner.

'I do a lot of Mozart concerti from the keyboard, because it's musically possible and musicologically correct and there's a precedent for it. I don't have the piano in the solo position. I stick it straight into the orchestra, so that the keyboard is on an absolute level with the concertmaster and either the first violas or the first cellos, depending on the setup. It's glorified chamber music. That's when you find out that you can conduct with a look, a nod, a reminder – anything. It helps if you play with an orchestra that either knows you or has had a history of doing this. For instance, right after Bernstein the New York Philharmonic did it very well. Now it's been awhile. Most of the orchestras enjoy it very much, for the reason I mentioned yesterday: they keep hoping you'll play terrible.' Laughter. 'You asked what else can be played. You can skip to the twentieth century – the nineteenth I wouldn't try. I remember once, a long, long time ago, hearing, of all people, Iturbi do the Tchaikovsky from the keyboard.' A whistle and a 'Whew!' from two of the students. 'That was about twenty-five years ago, and I think the orchestra just finished yesterday. It was unbelievable. There was no *semblance* of ensemble. On the other hand, I heard Mitropoulos when I was a kid do the Prokofiev Three. Phenomenal. I would hate to try it, but it's possible. I've done Shostakovich; obviously the Gershwin works, Ravel.'

A student asked, 'How about the Beethoven Triple?'

Previn said, 'The Beethoven *Triple*?' He shook his head. 'I haven't done that. I've played the piano in that, but, no, it wouldn't occur to me.' It's a notoriously difficult piece for all three soloists. 'Beethoven One, Two, Three would work. Four, Five – no. I wouldn't think so. What else?'

There were no suggestions from the students.

Previn went on, 'Strangely enough, the pieces that have the fewest orchestral problems in terms of number of notes are the most impossible to do. The Chopin concertos, for example – for which I sometimes think you need two conductors and a pianist.' Laughter. 'And Schumann, and all that. It's hopeless.'

A student asked, 'How about the Brahms Second?'

Previn said, 'Oh, no! God Almighty! No!' Laughter. 'Are you a pianist?' The student said yes, and Previn said, 'I don't mean this as a put-down, but try the Brahms Second and let me know how you make out. There are moments – the part with the clarinets, and the whole business with the cello – when the conductor just stands there anyway. But no. That's a terribly dangerous piece. And Brahms One is even worse.'

A student asked, 'If you rehearsed a *good* symphony – say, the Pittsburgh – in a big piece, a Mahler or a Tchaikovsky, let the concertmaster give the downbeat, and then had nobody conducting, what would happen?'

Previn said, 'I had an actual experience with that, and I did it on purpose. Several years ago, I did a show on the BBC in London called "Who Needs a Conductor?" because I found that a great number of very well-educated, very intelligent friends of mine asked that question. And they based it on a series of equations that were, roughly: the orchestra members are all professional and they've played it hundreds of times; the music is printed, and it's unalterable; metres are prescribed. Who needs you? So I wrote a show about that. At the beginning of the show, I started Beethoven Five and got them past the fermatas. I then left the podium and sat in the audience. During the filming of that show, I had two alternative points in mind. One point, in case they actually could do it, was to try to explain how and why. And I had another point to make in case they couldn't – and, thank God, they couldn't.' Laughter. 'Because after a while it got terribly rockety and raggedy. The first point would have been that time-beating is one thing, conducting another. In terms of time-beating, I think that an orchestra could probably keep together for a long time, if that's the question. But interpretatively I don't think you'd get unanimity of thought.'

A student asked, 'Wouldn't that depend on the kind of training they've had?'

Previn said, 'Yes, but you can carry that to extremes. The most "trained" orchestra I've ever heard is the old Cleveland, and I doubt very much if it would have occurred to those players to do a big piece and leave it totally alone. You see, the mental processes of all the players would be so channelled into simply staying together that all the supposedly higher aims of the music would have to go into second position, because the musicians would have absolutely nothing to hang on to but their own listening, and it can turn into a stunt rather than a performance. I may have overstated, in a way, that sometimes we're not necessary. That's true, and it's a good thing to remember. But it's also healthy to remember that most of the time we're *very* necessary for a good performance. Otherwise, why are we all struggling so to do it?'

A student asked, 'During a performance, do you think a conductor should give *more* emotionally or back off a bit? Also, is the orchestra more excited, up?'

'I can, of course, answer that only from a personal point

of view. During a concert, my attitude is one that I can't foresee. I don't *plan* to give more or to give less. Things happen. It's the same with the orchestra. That's why live music can't be duplicated; that's why, no matter how terrific records are, they're not the same. You ask me whether an orchestra suddenly comes "up", or back to life, or whatever, during a performance. Yes, of course it does. So do we. So, suddenly, the interplay is not one of "Remember, I'm going to do a rallentando!" but becomes one of making music together. And so your own adrenaline will either rise or fall, not necessarily by the evening but by the movement, by the phrase, by the bar. I wouldn't try to plan it if I were you. Just let it happen. Sometimes. . .'

He paused. 'Once, I was conducting a Brahms symphony, and I'd had a piece of very disturbing private news that day. I went out and really loosed it all on that symphony, and when it was over I thought, "Boy, that was really terrific." I went off, drenched and happy, into the wings, and my manager, for whom I've worked for twenty years, was standing there, and he said, "Would you mind telling me what that was all about just now?" I said, "Why?" And he said, "That was the most *disgraceful* exhibition of vulgar music-making I've ever heard." I was very angry with him. But I heard the tapes a few days later, and he was absolutely right. Because I'd had the conceit to think that my private worries were on a level with Brahms's language. And I tried to superimpose them on the music. And that kind of arrogance doesn't work.'

A hand went up. 'We hear about the Philadelphia "sound", the Chicago "sound". I'm not sure I know exactly what's meant. Since you've conducted both, I thought maybe you could explain it.'

Previn said, 'If I may, I'll give you two answers. The Philadelphia Orchestra is a very string-based orchestra. Chicago is brass-based. Two different approaches to a piece. And they've played that way for many years. On the other hand, I wouldn't want it said that an orchestra of mine had a specific sound, because I can't see making the same sound for Mahler and Elliot Carter. The sound has to change according to what you're playing. If it's always the same immenseness or the same languourousness, then there's something wrong. The Philadelphia knocks you *flat* when you conduct it. Unbelievable. And Chicago, too, in a different way. And Boston. But you can temper that sound according to the piece being played, though there are conductors who don't: Here I am in Chicago – *whack*!' Laughter. 'I don't think so. What many of us do is programme things that we, personally, would enjoy doing with that orchestra. When I went to Chicago, I did "The Rite of Spring". It was like standing in front of a Concorde. And in Philadelphia it's the "Alpine" Symphony. It's terrific. And if you multiply that by many conductors you get a continuous aiming at the sound the orchestras are supposed to have made in the past. These days, the music director isn't around that much, so you get a variety of conductors, with a variety of approaches, a variety of personal repertoires. A one-man band – which used to be the case, and has a lot to be said for it – is almost impossible to have now, as the world gets smaller, and more and more people stand in front of an orchestra. It's hard to keep one musical profile.'

A hand went up. 'Is there a preference in doing a lot of guest-conducting or in having your own orchestra?'

Previn said, 'While you're in an ascending spiral of learning repertoire and getting experience, if you can have the luxury of standing in front of the same people, getting musical and personal rapport with them, so they will bear with you while you learn the repertoire, you're better off than you would be running around, facing at least partially recalcitrant groups. An interviewer's favourite question is "Isn't it difficult facing a different group?" Well, it's much more difficult for the orchestra to face a different conductor. So I think until you can say, "That programme doesn't bother me so much because it has a Beethoven or a Brahms or a Mozart or a Haydn", meaning there are no preparation problems, until you get to that

127

point, if you can work with an orchestra, even if it's imbalanced, with technical problems, you're better off. But when you're in a position where your career has not yet reached its apex, *anything* you get to conduct is terrific – your own orchestra or somebody else's, a rehearsal, anything. I have not yet done a rehearsal of a piece, even if I've done it two hundred and fifty times, that hasn't taught me something. Never. Certain tricks of the trade are not reprehensible at all. Suppose you're with Orchestra X and somebody says, "That's a terrible page-turn." The next time you do that piece let the orchestra know you know this. And if you come on a bowing that works a dream, spring it on the next orchestra. They'll look at you with admiration, which is perfectly all right.'

Miss Deutsch said, 'Some of us have conducted only chamber orchestras. Do you have any advice about approaching bigger repertoire – tone poems, Mahler? There's *so* much.'

Previn said, 'It's not a bad idea to pick one that, at that point in your life, you adore – that you can't do without. Do it twenty times. And if you hear something you're absolutely wild about, learn it. When you love a piece, the orchestra will react. Sometimes we do pieces that we respect but don't love, and there's a big difference in the performance. Sometimes you'll hear an extremely respectful performance of the *German Requiem*. It's better when the conductor adores it.'

Meier glanced at his watch, and Previn concluded, 'If instead of making music you think about it, fantasise about it, that's a lost day. Down the drain, and you'll never recapture it. When you're involved with music, it makes you very happy, and when you lose that – as some of my colleagues have done in their later years – you're in big trouble. I must tell you, I've never cheated on music – never. Sometimes the work grind dulls the edge of that voracious affair we all have with music. It's sad when that happens. The longer you can avoid that, the better. I think you have to be in love with music every day.'

Part III

CHAPTER 1

Compared with the rhapsodic reviews Previn often gets in England and in Europe, American critics tend to be somewhat cool toward him, and it's not at all unusual that Pittsburgh's two music critics, Robert Croan and Carl Apone, of the Pittsburgh *Post-Gazette* and the *Pittsburgh Press*, respectively, after an initial burst of enthusiasm when Previn took over for William Steinberg, gradually began to be picky about the Pittsburgh's performances and Previn's programming. Local critics in this country simply are that way with a resident music director. In Boston, Michael Steinberg, of the Boston *Globe*, was so hard not only on Seiji Ozawa but nearly every guest conductor that when he quit the *Globe* the symphony management heaved a sigh of relief and promptly hired him to write programme notes – an art at which he is, in many people's opinion, unparalleled. Steinberg's successor, Richard Dyer, is critical, too, though without Steinberg's terrible venom. Also, Dyer's criticism is tempered by an almost tangible love of music.

In November of 1981, Previn and the Pittsburgh performed three programmes of English music in both of New York's big halls – Carnegie and Avery Fisher – for a mini–tour called the British Festival. There were two concerts in Carnegie Hall, and Donal Henahan of the *New York Times* reviewed the first concert. Henahan has mellowed since he came to the *Times* from Claudia Cassidy country in Chicago, and his reviews often reflect the joy in music and a benevolent attitude toward struggling performers. (He succeeded Harold Schonberg as the Number One critic of the *Times*, and his essays in the Arts and Leisure Section are witty and informative and apt to propel a non-music-lover to a concert.) Of the first concert he

131

wrote, 'André Previn led his Pittsburgh Symphony Orchestra into Carnegie Hall for the first of two concerts in a British Festival that gave every prospect of cementing artistic relations between England and the United States, and perhaps between Pittsburgh and New York as well. The program even included a greeting to America from one Margaret Thatcher of 10 Downing Street.' Henahan did not much care for the music, but he noted the improved quality of the Pittsburgh orchestra 'both in its solo players and in ensemble cohesion' and the 'full, pure, and velvety' sounds of its strings. John Rockwell, also of the *New York Times*, reviewed the third concert, in Avery Fisher Hall. (A lot of performers ask friends to scout the hall, to find out which *Times* critic, if any, is sitting in the aisle seat. When it's Rockwell, the performers wince.) Rockwell was highly visible in his aisle seat, mimicking Previn's conducting gestures for a friend throughout the concert. Rockwell proclaimed, 'The Pittsburgh Symphony seems an honorable but not distinguished orchestra.' Andrew Porter, writing in *The New Yorker*, took his colleagues to task. He quoted from the two reviews and said,

I'd put it rather more warmly than that, and rate the orchestra above, say, the New York Philharmonic, if somewhere below the Chicago Symphony and the Philadelphia. The Pittsburgh string tone was certainly fuller, warmer, more 'singing' than we New Yorkers hear except at the Met and from the best visitors. The woodwinds did not draw attention away from the music onto individual virtuoso prowess, but the episodes of important solo work – the alto flute's duetting with the solo violin in the Tippett concerto, the English horn in the romanza of Vaughan Williams' Fifth Symphony – lacked neither their accomplishment nor eloquence. The brasses never blared out, as Chicago brasses can, to stun us and swamp their colleagues on the platform. Most important – and the hardest to describe – was the 'feel' of an orchestra that loves and believes in the music it plays, that seeks to communicate its enjoyment, that listens and makes the audience listen, too. In short, Mr Previn has, to judge by these concerts, led the Pittsburgh Symphony into America's top orchestra league.

Present at the New York concerts were the Previn children who live in New York with their mother: Fletcher, Daisy, Lark, and Soon-Yi. Whenever Previn came to New York, Fletcher would stay with him at the Regency, and at a brief reception following the last Avery Fisher concert Fletcher, dressed in a grey flannel suit with short pants, held his father's baton. Previn had breakfast and lunch with all the children, and usually managed to give a concert at their school, too, whenever he was in the city.

Also in 1981, Previn got his associate conductor, the Englishman Michael Lankester. Lankester had been one of four finalists in an international conducting competition in London, but he had not won. Previn, one of the judges, had favoured Lankester, and after the name of the winner was announced Previn sought Lankester out and told him not to be discouraged. Lankester, a sandy-haired handsome man in his mid-thirties, told me, 'When *Every Good Boy Deserves Favour* became a hit, and was in for a long run in London, André asked me to conduct the orchestra, and when that came to an end he let me conduct the LSO in rehearsals, and then he even shared some concerts with me.' (Lankester was one of the three conductors that Previn had told the students in Tanglewood about.)

Lankester had, of course, come along with the Pittsburgh on the tour. An associate conductor learns all the scores, and if anything should happen to the conductor he must be prepared to step in. There are some aspects of touring that musicians love, one being favourite restaurants in cities that have become familiar over the years, and after the Avery Fisher concert Pittsburgh players had scattered before the last of the audience members had left the hall. The Pittsburgh's managing director, Marshall Turkin, invited Lankester to have a drink with him. He said, 'We will go to my club.' Lankester got into a cab with Turkin and watched from the cab window as the city and then its skyline vanished from his view. He was taken out to La Guardia Airport's TWA Ambassador Lounge – Turkin's 'club' – for a drink.

When the orchestra played at the Kennedy Center, in Washington, DC, the second stop of the British Festival, Turkin saw Dinah Daniels backstage and said, 'What? You're still here?' Back in Pittsburgh, he fired her. She had had ten years' experience with the Boston Symphony, and Turkin had beseeched her to come to Pittsburgh to handle media relations. Miss Daniels is extremely bright and extraordinarily efficient, and she has an enthusiastic love of music that is reflected in the work she does in the field. Many people thought she was one of the best things to happen to the Pittsburgh in some time. Pressed for a reason for the dismissal, Turkin would only say, 'I've never met a woman who made me feel so uncomfortable.' Smart women, in general, seemed to affect him that way, and Kathleen Butera was removed from her job some time later by the simple act of Turkin's taking her title, and hence her job, away. Once Miss Butera, a native of Pittsburgh, was safely out of town and working for the San Diego Symphony, Turkin replaced her with a man, and gave him the job with a slightly different title and duties. When Previn talked to me in 1980 about all the hours he spent 'talking things into the ground with management', management meant Marshall Turkin.

In December of 1981, Previn and Turkin flew to New York to meet with John Duffy, the director of the 'Meet the Composer' programme. The programme is advertised in full-page ads in major magazines. The ad shows a photograph of a man, in shirtsleeves, seated at a piano, score paper in the rack, cup of coffee next to him, on the piano bench. The copy reads,

> Writing music is a labor of love. But for even the most celebrated composers, finding an orchestra to perform it can be a frustrating exercise. Now, thanks to an innovative program, we'll be hearing from contemporary composers more often. The 'Meet the Composer/Orchestra Residencies Program' places composers in two-year residencies with major orchestras throughout America. Each Composer-In-Residence works closely with the music director, acts as liaison between the orchestra and other composers, organizes concerts of new music and writes a major work to be premiered and recorded by the orchestra. This new program gives gifted and accomplished artists the chance to create a brighter future for today's music.

Turkin had told Previn that the composer would have to be a local man, a man whose music did not appeal greatly to Previn, but Previn was willing to try anything that would help him introduce more modern music to recalcitrant Pittsburgh audiences. He even hoped someday to have a separate modern-music series, so people could choose for themselves what they wanted to hear. He has said, 'As admirable as Boulez was – programming so much modern music in New York – what he did was unworkable. You simply cannot *cram* modern music down an audience's throat.'

In New York, at the Regency Hotel, Previn and Turkin met with John Duffy; Howard Klein, deputy director of Arts and Humanities for the Rockefeller Foundation; and Leonard Fleischer, senior arts advisor of the Exxon Corporation. Both men represented two of the programme's sponsors. The third sponsor was the National Endowment for the Arts. The programme that year was offered to seven selected cities, and Duffy, quite rightly, thought the first thing Previn should see was a list of the composers available to him. To Previn's surprise, the name of the Pittsburgh composer was not on the list. To his great delight, John Harbison was available. Previn chose Harbison, whose term in Pittsburgh would begin in the fall of 1982.

When Previn's friend Alan Jay Lerner married for the seventh or eighth time in the summer of 1980, Previn's eyes rounded in amazement at the news. He feels that divorce is one of life's most painful experiences, but on 4 January 1982, after three years of self-scrutiny, Previn married Heather Hales, a thirty-three-year-old divorcée with three children. The new Mrs Previn is English, and Previn told all of his friends that they were married in London, but he took her along when the Pittsburgh was in San Francisco on a tour of the western states in February, and Previn told his friend the columnist Herb Caen, of the San Francisco *Chronicle*, that they were married in Pittsburgh (a month before Previn was due back in that city). Previn said, 'You know how I am about privacy. Who else would fly to Pittsburgh in January to get married?' No, they did not go to Warsaw on their honeymoon. Heather Previn told Caen that she'd had a busy time: the day before, in Los Angeles, she'd met two ex-wives, a step-daughter, and her new mother-in-law. She'd made a hit with all four, and she'd done the same with the Board of Directors of the Pittsburgh Symphony. At a party held to give the board a chance to meet her, the board's president at the time, Robert J. Buckley, told her that he'd always wanted to own an English company, and he'd just bought one of that country's oldest and most distinguished, Wilkinson Sword. A shocked Mrs Previn said, 'I think that's a lot of bloody cheek', which tickled the phenomenally rich Mr Buckley – the CEO of Allegheny International – so much that he repeated what she said to him every chance he got.

In the spring of 1982, Previn took his orchestra on a three-week, twelve-city European tour that was a triumph from start to finish. There was not one bad review – as a matter of fact, the reviews, put together, read like a lexicon of superlatives. Orchestra members reported that, in their opinion, they had never played better, leading some people to surmise that the more receptive the audience, the better the performance.

In that year, too, it was announced that Previn would become the music director of the Royal Philharmonic Orchestra, in London. He would continue with the Pittsburgh, of course, and the new appointment, effective in the spring of 1985, would allow him even more time to be in Pittsburgh – time to keep an eye on things, even when he wasn't conducting. Since leaving the LSO, in 1979, he had been guest-conducting in Europe and America. As he put it, 'I was flying back and forth, the way some people go to the Hamptons.' Guest-conducting fees are high, but not worth the physical toll they take, except, perhaps, for a conductor's manager.

CHAPTER 2

In the summer of 1983 Previn came to Tanglewood again, this time for a month's stay. He rented a house on the outskirts of Lenox, and brought Heather and her three children – Tom, eleven; Ben, ten; and the adopted Vietnamese daughter, nine-year-old Li-an. (Previn's twins were now living in New York, with their mother, and going to school there. All of his children were on vacation in Connecticut, and he planned to spend a couple of weeks with them after he had completed his Tanglewood commitments.) During that month, Previn was scheduled to conduct the Boston Symphony Orchestra in three weekend concerts; conduct the Berkshire Music Center student orchestra in the Tchaikovsky fifth symphony; work with the student conductors at Seranak (they would be conducting the two pianists Seiji Ozawa hires each summer); coach students in the performance of chamber music; and play chamber music in several of Tanglewood's Prelude Concerts, which would include doing a Brahms sonata and the César Franck Sonata with Joseph Silverstein. In October of 1983, Previn would record six ninety-minute programmes with the Royal Philharmonic Orchestra on the development of the symphony for the BBC, and the programmes' producer, Herbert Chapple, was in Tanglewood. In Previn's spare time, he would work on the scripts for the programmes with Chapple.

When Previn greeted me at the door, he seemed a different man. Gone was the hunted, haunted, guarded look. In the glassed-in, two-storey living-room he introduced me to his wife.

Heather is a tall, striking woman, with auburn hair, worn shoulder-length, with bangs. She has high cheekbones, a pert nose, the kind of complexion Englishwomen

138

are famous for, an open, friendly manner, and brown eyes that, at times, reflect a delicious, wicked sense of humour. She was gently, roundly pregnant, and was wearing a blue denim jumper over a white T-shirt. She was working on a needlepoint pillowcase – big alphabet letters in pink and blue. Hanging from a lamp in the corner were two mobiles: red plastic clothes hangers with multi-coloured yarn dangling from the bars. Something nice for a baby to grab at.

Previn said, 'We went to a party the kids had – the student conductors and the orchestra – last night, and Heather danced with *everyone*. She danced all night.' He looked amazed. He told me about another party they had gone to the previous Sunday – brunch at the home of William Bernell, who is the artistic administrator of the BSO. Thomas Morris is the orchestra's general manager. (General managers, managing directors, executive directors – the titles vary. Sometimes vice-president is attached. They are go-betweens for the board and the music director, and only rarely can they please both. Ozawa and Morris clashed about a number of things, and Bernell was hired to be the conductor's and the general manager's go-between.) Ozawa was at the brunch, and so was his personal masseuse. Conductors tend to be long-lived, many feel because of the unique, constant exercise they get – all that arm-waving. (The syndicated columnist Joe Hyams once hired a football star to wave his arms for the entire length of a Brahms symphony. The football player, exhausted, had to quit long before the symphony had ended – an indication that if the brain, or the intelligence, is not engaged, conducting is a bigger physical strain than anyone had previously realised.) Ozawa's masseuse worked him over daily, and this Sunday he urged Previn to try it – it felt great. Previn, flat on the floor, face down, didn't think it felt great. Heather Previn looked on as the masseuse walked all over her husband's back while everyone else present ate bacon and eggs. Previn thought the ordeal was over, but the masseuse flipped him over and said,

139

'Now, *Bartók*!' In retrospect, he was amused, but he didn't want a masseuse all his own.

When Silverstein asked Previn which Brahms sonata he would like to play, Previn, characteristically, picked the only one of the three he had never done before – the A-Major. Later in the day, he was going to meet Silverstein in the Shed for a first rehearsal, and he excused himself and went upstairs to practice. Heather put the needlepoint aside, and went into the kitchen to make some tea. The living-room was furnished with soft beige love seats, facing each other and perpendicular to a large flagstone fireplace that on this particular day looked obscene. Tanglewood was having its annual heat wave, and the house, to the terrible discomfort of the Previns, was not air-conditioned. (Previn had said, 'It's perfect for *skiers*, for Christ's sake!') The living-room overlooked a redwood deck, a meadow, and the blue Berkshires in the distance.

Heather returned with two mugs of tea, which she put on a glass coffee table, between the love seats, and sat down opposite me. I asked her to tell me something about herself, and she said, 'I was born in Oxford – the heart of learning. Much good it did me!' She laughed at herself. 'My father, Robert Sneddon, was a diplomat in the British Embassy; he's now retired. My childhood was spent going all around Europe. We lived in Berlin, and in Bonn, and in Oslo, Stockholm, Prague, Paris – all the capital cities that one dreams about. I used to be multi-lingual, but through lack of use I'm not anymore, though my French is fairly fluent. I used to speak Polish, but that's completely gone. I would love to have used Polish to learn Russian with, but we never got to Russia. I never learned German – I found it an impossible language. I feel more Scandinavian than English, because I spent all my formative years there – from three to fourteen. I have a sister who is seven years younger than I am. We're good friends now, but our interests didn't gel until I was twenty-five and she was seventeen. I'm very close to my parents; my mother's name is Kay. They're the best people in the world, and we

140

all have a very close relationship – including André. They live in Surrey, too – about a thirty-minute drive from us.'

In the *New York Times*'s announcement of the Previns' marriage, Heather was said to be a 'glass etcher', and I asked her how she got into it.

She said, 'Actually, it's engraving, which is quite a different thing. Etching involves the use of acid, to burn out the surface of the glass. I'd always fiddled with painting and drawing, but I wasn't very good at applying colour. I made a horrible mess with paint, and I got tired of just doing pencil sketches. I wanted to do something a little bit different – a little outré, I suppose. I read about this incredible man named Laurence Whistler, who was a poet and an artist, and a glass engraver. When he started glass engraving, it had lain dormant for about three hundred years. I thought that would be the best thing for me, because I could learn the engraving, and the glass would provide the colour. You have light, so you're playing with light as well. It was marvellous for me. I don't do it anymore, because I don't have the proper facilities at home. Glass is a dangerous medium, in that as you engrave you're stirring up a lot of dust and breathing in lead crystals, and you have to be able to wash it away as you work. You can't have a moving studio: you have to have a place that is always there, ready for working, because glass is heavy and fragile, and you also have to be able to lock it against children. And any wandering itinerant who might come in.' She paused and laughed. 'You have to do it all against black, so you can see the engraving as you do it. My studio at home was completely black, all around, which was slightly sinister but absolutely necessary. I really loved doing it. I got commissions from people, which I preferred to mass production. People have very little imagination about what to put on glass. Clients wanted their baby's initials and date of birth, which is fine. But I loved the big, heraldic pieces. Doing something for a guild, for instance – their coat of arms.' She said that although she loved doing it, it created a great deal of anxiety, and the biggest anxiety attack she had had involved a piece she did for Previn. 'The LSO commissioned me to do something commemorating his tenth anniversary with the orchestra. He had countless silver batons, and the orchestra wanted to present him with something different. The choice of what I would do was left to me. I considered and dismissed a plate or a goblet. I hunted around, and I found an *enormous* piece of rough lead crystal at Whitefriars – thirty pounds.' While she was talking, an exquisite little girl came downstairs and into the living-room. She had black hair, pink cheeks, and blue eyes. Heather said to me, 'This is Li-an', and to the child, 'You can stay, but you mustn't talk right now.' Li-an snuggled up next to her mother, who put her arm around her.

Heather continued, 'This huge piece is absolutely clear to look at – like a piece of ice. There's no flaw anywhere. The edges are jagged – like an iceberg. It has three clean, clear facets on it. I discussed it with the LSO, and they decided they wanted their logo, a bit of writing to commemorate the anniversary, with their name and André's name and the date; and on the biggest facet they wanted the first six bars of the Hadyn "London" Symphony. I glibly said, "Oh, no trouble at all." It had to be all freehand. I put it off and I put it off. Every time I saw this pristine piece of glass and thought about what I had to do my hands would shake. I had to do the stave with no ruler! I kept thinking, "What if I screw up? What if the stave is wiggly?" ' She told me that she procrastinated until she had less than three days to complete the project and deliver it in time for the celebration dinner. One night she went to bed, and at three in the morning she woke and said to herself, 'Now.' She got up, drank a mug of coffee, and did the stave lines perfectly. She said, 'What a relief! That thirty-pound hunk of lead crystal cost a *fortune.*'

A handsome blond boy appeared in the doorway, and Heather introduced him to me. 'This is my son Ben. My other son, Tom, is swimming in a neighbour's pool.' Ben asked her what the word 'debonair' meant.

Heather said, 'Sophisticated, dashing. Your father is debonair.'

Ben asked, 'Which one?' and Heather laughed and said, 'Daddy Michael. Your father.'

Ben asked, 'Isn't André debonair?' and Heather said, 'I just don't think of him that way.'

Ben persisted. He asked, 'Is Jimmy Carter debonair?' We both laughed at that. Heather said, 'I wouldn't think so. David Niven is debonair.' That seemed to satisfy Ben, and he thanked her and went back upstairs.

Heather returned to the subject of the lead-crystal trophy. She said, 'That was 1978, I believe. I'd been divorced a year, and it was a difficult time. My ex-husband is a lovely man, and we're good friends, but our marrying was one of the biggest mistakes of both our lives. We got along like a house on fire, but we weren't cut out to be married. It was difficult, the responsibility of raising three children, because he went off *instantly* to marry another lady, and of course his mind and his thoughts were with her. I took a very, very back seat for quite a while. Being totally alone, without any reference to another adult, it was hard for me. I was pretty *angry*, but mostly with myself, for not being able to hang it all together. Now I'm glad I didn't.'

Heather Previn's ex-husband is the actor Michael Jayston (he was Nicholas in *Nicholas and Alexander*), and he'd done two films with Mia Farrow. The Jaystons were house-hunting, and Miss Farrow invited them to live in the Previns' guest cottage. Jayston and Miss Farrow were making another film, and while they were working Heather looked for a house. She said, 'I found one in a couple of months, and in the course of that period we all became good friends. Occasionally, schedules permitting, we went out together. Michael asked for a divorce in 1977, and some time later Mia and André broke up. A year or so after that, André called and invited me to Wimbledon, and

143

I went, not expecting *any thing* at all. It was just a relief to go somewhere without the children, with someone I knew and liked a lot. We enjoyed each other's company. He made me laugh, which I hadn't done in a long time, and I think I made *him* laugh, and it went then from strength to strength. He was the last person in the world I could have imagined for myself. After I'd been seeing him for perhaps six months, my mother said, "Do you enjoy each other's company?" and I said, "Oh, yes", like the dutiful daughter. She asked, "Do you laugh a lot?" and I said, "All the time. We seem to find something funny in every situation", and she said, "Oh, dear. That's bad." She's a wise woman, and she wanted to protect me. André had a reputation of being something of a rascal. But he's a *lovely* rascal. I recommend rascals.' She laughed, and added, 'I have him and Mia to thank for Li-an. They vouched for Michael and me when we adopted her.' She gave Li-an a hug. She said, 'When Michael and I were divorced, I wanted a name of my own choosing. I'd always had to spell my maiden name for people, and I chose for my new legal name my favourite grandmother's maiden name – a happy name, Hales.'

The rascal had finished practising, and came in, yawning and stretching. He said, 'That Brahms is a bitch, but I wanted to play it with Joey. He's done every chamber-music piece hundreds of times, and I always learn something from him.'

One friend of Previn's said that Previn had his foot in so many things that at times he seemed to be tap dancing. I'd heard that at one time he'd been the director of the prestigious South Bank Music Festival, and I asked him about it now.

He said, 'I did it for two years. Everybody – Barenboim, Marriner, Pinky, Simon Rattle – had it for the same period. It's very time-consuming. Every night for six weeks. It was a terrific series, because you could take the *wildest* chances. It was great fun. I really confused the issues, because we had extremely serious chamber-music concerts,

and then one night a week we took gambles. One night there was a premiere of a string quartet of Nicholas Maw, and then Dizzy Gillespie played with his quartet. I based one programme on improvisation. There was a man at the BBC, whose name I've forgotten, who had an encyclopedic knowledge of film. I asked him to compile a half hour of silent films, which should be totally non-sequiturial, where one sequence *never* leads to the next, with insane flashes of things that lasted ten seconds and never came again. He did this, and I got Richard Rodney Bennett, who is a *wonderful* composer and a very good pianist. Neither one of us saw the film in advance, and in front of a packed Festival Hall I set up two pianos, and I had a genius percussionist – a renowned instrumentalist and composer named Stomu Yamashti – who used countless instruments. The three of us, in front of the audience, watched this film unreel, where *nothing* ever made any sense, and we improvised a score. A lot of it was extremely atonal, very wild, and there was a sudden moment, in the middle of a Biblical scene, of a man and a woman in the early twenties lighting up cigarettes and inhaling *deeply*, and Rodney and I, by insane joke instinct, in the same split second and in the same key, played "Tea for Two". It brought the house down. Another night – I had discovered in *Grove's* Dictionary that Richard Strauss wrote an hour-long piano accompaniment score to the entire poem *Enoch Arden*. I couldn't believe that he'd done that. Through a German-archive library, I got the music, and I hired some actors from the Royal Shakespeare Company and a wonderful director, Buzz Goodbody, who assigned parts. We did *Enoch Arden* as a Victorian melodrama, and I played the Strauss score onstage. Ben Kingsley played Enoch Arden.'
Heather said, 'And I was carousing and drinking in the Opera Tavern, *hearing* about *Enoch Arden* being done on the South Bank.'
Previn said, 'We started out doing it as a put-on, because the music was lush and the plot so melodramatic. But after the rehearsal Buzz said, "They will scream with

laughter for the first five minutes, and for the next fifty-five the audience will turn into corpses. Actors never get to do a Victorian play without setting it up. Do it straight." She was right. The actors *and* the audience loved it.'

Heather got involved with the Rehabilitation Institute of Pittsburgh, an organisation that has done remarkable work with handicapped children. In November of 1982, Previn planned a fund-raiser for the Institute. He told me, 'For the fund-raiser I did not want to ask the orchestra to play for two reasons: I didn't want to ask a favour of that many people, and since they play in the hall so regularly, it wouldn't be a novelty. There's a terrific promoter in Florida who said that there are only five absolute box-office guarantees in the classical world today, and four of them are Itzhak Perlman. So I asked Itzhak. We were going to do a programme of sonatas, but there was an illness in his family, and he had to cancel. So with twenty-four hours' notice, and the house sold out – two hundred and fifty dollars a ticket – out of sheer desperation I called two of my old jazz friends in California and New York, and true to their code they said "Sure", and played for a plane ticket. Shelly Manne on drums and Monty Budwig on bass. Heather is on the board now, and she was asked to be the master of ceremonies, so to speak. She had a very sweet reticence about going out onstage and talking to three thousand people; she was *so* nervous that I went out with her. I told the audience, "I'm just here to keep my wife company", and I sat down to the rear of the rostrum. She did very well. She was charming and funny and informative. When she got to the end of the prepared text, her hands began to shake' – Heather interjected, 'Don't forget the knees' – 'and I got up, took her hand, and said, "Say good night, Gracie", George Burns's radio-programme sign-off quip to his twittering wife, Gracie, and we walked off together.' Both Pittsburgh papers pronounced the concert a complete success, and both quoted Previn as having said, in advance, that he would rather be hung by his thumbs than play jazz in public. The trio's only 'rehearsal' was a list of some tunes written on the back of a ticket stub. Previn said, when they had finished playing, 'I keep thinking that when I go outside it's going to be 1958 again.' He glanced at his watch and got up to get his music. He said, 'I'm coming back here for the full season next summer. I'll be on six months' sabbatical, starting in January, and I don't think it's fair to conduct a major orchestra when I'm not conducting the Pittsburgh, so I won't conduct the BSO. I'll just work with the students. I've been asked to do a documentary of the Berkshire Music Center for the BBC – a great idea. I'll do that next summer, too.' He added, 'The student orchestra this year is so sensational that I tried to arrange to take them on tour. But it wasn't possible. They come from *everywhere*.' He said it was time for him to go to the Shed to rehearse with Silverstein, and the three of us went out to their rented station wagon, which was parked on the gravel turn-in to their house. Heather had the keys, but Previn took them from her and said he would drive. Out on the road, his hand resting affectionately on her knee, he drove on the left side. She reminded him that he was not in England, and he switched to the right lane.

Heather said to me, 'He's a terrible driver', and he said, somewhat smugly, 'I have *never* had an accident.'

Heather said, 'But in your wake, you leave three-car collisions.'

CHAPTER 3

The Shed backstage has cement-block walls, a cement floor, and bright-orange walls with numbered doors indicating the practice rooms. Previn led the way to No. 1, which he knew had the best piano, but Peter Serkin was in there, practising Peter Lieberson's piano concerto, which would be premiered at the Saturday-night concert. Previn and Silverstein went to the next-best piano, in room No. 4. When great musicians meet to rehearse, there is often an air of excitement, anticipation, a feeling that they're breathing not oxygen but helium. And so it was today.

When Previn rehearsed with Silverstein and his BSO colleagues on previous occasions, Previn was amused at all the joking that went on. But Silverstein, who was the leader of the Boston for twenty-two years and an assistant conductor for thirteen years, now had his own orchestra, the Utah Symphony, brought to jewel quality by Maurice Abravanal, its music director for almost forty years. Abravanal retired for reasons of health, and Silverstein became the new music director. (At the end of the 1984 Tanglewood season, he severed all ties with the BSO, and moved his family to Salt Lake City.) The talk today was more concerned with conducting than joking.

Silverstein is a handsome, even-featured, gentle man. He is soft-spoken, surprisingly, for a man of such dazzling virtuosity and with the character and conviction necessary to be a leader of a great orchestra.

While Silverstein was tuning, they talked.

Previn said, 'You know whose music I used to quite like, and then he got lost? Harold Shapero.'

Silverstein said, 'He just simply stopped writing. We were neighbours for quite a while.' (Possibly coincidentally,

148

Silverstein performed a sonata of Shapero's at Tanglewood the following summer.)

They began with the Franck, in A-major, which opens with a wistful, pensive melody in the violin. The theme, which becomes more assertive, is taken over by the piano, riding on light chords, and as Previn played he said, 'Do you want me to go ahead on this?' Silverstein said, 'Sure.' When he wasn't playing he sang along with Previn. There are a lot of rubatos in that sonata, and he stopped singing and said, 'You can pick a flower on every third beat, if you like.'

When they'd finished the first climactic section, Previn said, 'I think it's nice what you do. You move it a bit. When it's played too reverentially, it dies.'

Silverstein said, 'You have to pick and choose your spots with this one, or else it becomes notey.'

They continued to play, and Silverstein said, 'You can give me a little more sound there.' As they played, he said, 'Now it's too Wagnerian', and Previn laughed and dropped down a bit. (When Previn plays jazz, he leans over the keyboard and really goes at it; he is quite different with classical music. There's a set to his shoulders that seems to free his arms and his hands, and he looks absolutely nonchalant playing what a Juilliard pianist might call a 'knuckle buster'.)

When they'd finished, Previn said, 'You know, this first movement takes a *gigantic* hand. Look at this', and he played a chord.

Silverstein said, 'Do you suppose he just expected people to arpeggiate those things?'

Previn said, 'There are certain moments where you can't do anything else. He must have been *enormous*.' Silverstein lit a cigarette, and Previn said, 'Did you ever play the Ives Sonata? I love the instructions. It says, "Play whatever is possible." ' Silverstein chuckled, and Previn added, 'And the Schumann "Toccata". It says, "Play as fast as possible" – he played the Schumann as he talked – 'and then "Play faster." '

Silverstein said, 'Thanks a lot.'

The second movement of the Franck is very fast and a terrible task for the pianist. Previn said, 'I don't know how I'll make out without a page-turner, but I'll do my best.' The violin begins on the G-string – a passionate, agitated theme. Silverstein had said, 'I'm not gutsy enough for this, really', but he is and was. The middle section is tinged with poignancy, and Previn said, 'Does it get slower? Or did I do something?' Silverstein said, 'Sure it gets slower. It kind of drifts down.' Previn flipped pages back to the beginning of the movement. He said, 'So you really want a hell of a tempo here.' Silverstein said yes, and added, 'Otherwise, the tune doesn't make too much sense. All that figuration gets too specific for my taste.' The two were well-matched in musicianship and virtuosity, and sitting there listening I felt sorry for all the people who would hear them play in the huge, open Shed, and not with this immediacy. They continued, and the theme builds and builds, moving into higher registers, step by step, and reaches a peak, and suddenly Silverstein dropped to a pianissimo, catching Previn off guard. Previn said, 'Oh, *ho*!' He laughed. '*Right*! That's *nice*!' They finished, and Previn noodled at a passage. He said, 'I can't get those goddam low Bs on this piano. It's frustrating.' The bad piano reminded him of another bad piano, and he said, 'We were on a run-out [a concert in a nearby city] with the Pittsburgh, and I was playing a Mozart. The piano was hopeless; there was no way for the orchestra to tune to it. The whole orchestra groaned when they heard the first two notes. In the middle of the first movement, Fritz Siegal leaned over and said to me, "You've *got* to learn to play in tune." '

Silverstein laughed, and said, 'A great party record is one I have of the Saint-Saëns Third Symphony that we did up here on a very *hot* Sunday. We can't hear the organ onstage, because the pipes are up in the clouds. It *did* sound a little weird to me, and when I came off the stage the guys in the broadcast both were on the *floor*.' The heat

150

had affected the intonation of the organ radically, and Silverstein played for Previn how it had sounded, landing on minor, out-of-tune, jarring thirds loudly.

Previn laughed, and said, 'That piece is *anathema* to me. I know everybody wants to conduct it.'

Silverstein said, 'There's a wonderful English word – "treacly" – and that piece is treacly. When the organ comes in at the A-flat-major place, I'm tempted to say, "Dearly beloved . . ." '

Previn said, 'The *all-time* Victorian organ entrance is in the "Alpine" Symphony, but that's nice. With the trumpet solo on top of it. Jesus.'

Silverstein said, 'That great passage in the Mahler Three' – he sang it – 'if you're not in the mood for that – ' Previn said, 'Conversely, if you *are*, it will put you on the floor.'

Silverstein added, 'It's very, very touching. It's just hovering on the brink.'

They were so caught up in the third movement – free, contemplative, the violin following introductory piano chords, the theme passing back and forth between the two instruments, and then the two are together – that there was no talking.

The last movement is a joyous canon that ends with a trill and a long run in the piano and one final note in the violin. Silverstein said, 'You know what Jascha does', and Previn grinned and said, 'Yeah, sure.' Silverstein explained to me, 'He plays the run along with the piano. He couldn't stand to be left out.'

Previn said, 'I like that tempo. It's comfortable.' He flipped pages back and looked at the beginning of the movement. He said, 'It's amazing. This piece can be played in a million ways. I did it with Kyung-Wha Chung seven years ago. She had *so* many things – all justifiable, but completely different.' Cellists have been including the Franck on solo programmes, in transcription, for many years, and now Previn said, 'Did you hear the record Jimmy Galway made of this?'

151

Silverstein laughed a laugh that sounded more like a snort. 'Rampal did it, too. Actually, he was the original criminal who took the piece over.' He lit a cigarette and said, 'I did the Franck Symphony up here three summers ago with the orchestra. It was the first time it had been played here in *eighteen* years.'

Previn said, 'That's a piece I can do without,' and Silverstein said, 'If you take a look at it again, and are far enough removed from the clichés of our childhood, if you put the piece together and don't belabour every possible nuance, every possible rubato, it's quite lovely.'

Previn said, 'But once you start counting the chromaticisms, it's out of the question.'

Included in the Boston Symphony's Saturday-night concert was Franck's 'Le Chausseur Maudit' ('The Accursed Hunter'), and now Silverstein reminisced about the time Charles Munch, who had been an integral part of the Tanglewood scene for many years, conducted that symphonic poem, and how he spoke to the orchestra. Silverstein was laughing as he spoke. He imitated the famed conductor's thick French accent: 'I *can't* tell you the story of this piece. It is a *terrible* story. But I *must* tell you the story!'

Previn said, 'I once heard him do a "La Mer" and all you heard was a whirring sound. Nothing left of the notes, but it was fabulous!'

Silverstein said, 'We did play, on several occasions, the Second Suite from "Daphnis" in under fourteen minutes.'

Previn said, 'But that's very un-French – to do it that fast.' Silverstein said, 'It's more Alsatian.' Previn said, 'Charlie Dutoit does it at that speed. It goes like a bat. We both recorded the complete suite at the same time. We had an argument about it. I believe you should actually hear everything, which is slower than you think, and his is faster than you think. But, of course, his will fracture everyone who hears it, because it's *phenomenal*.' Silverstein said, 'Well, if you're going to go for that, that's one aesthetic. Another approach is, if you look at a score that's

152

extremely dense and marvellously put together and if you really enjoy the craft of the piece. . .' Previn said, 'I like to hear all those little percussion things. But his is terrific.'

Silverstein asked, 'How are things working out with John Harbison?' Previn said, '*Very* well.' Silverstein said, 'He's a first-class musician', and Previn said, 'Do you know his fiddle concerto?'

Silverstein said, 'Yes. I plan to perform it out West in the fall.'

He tuned, and they turned to the Brahms A-Major Sonata, the second of the three sonatas that the composer wrote for violin and piano. The first four notes are from the *Meistersinger*. The piano begins and the violin answers. They went straight through without stopping, and finished the movement. Previn said, 'For the moment, let's go on.'

The second movement opens with a sweetly sad andante followed, startlingly, by a fast scherzo, which has pizzicato double-stops in the violin, staccato chords in the piano, with Brahms's signature syncopation throughout. Silverstein said, 'If we play it right, there's a kind of inevitability about it.' He added, 'These rhythms are so hard that if you don't have the right pulse, it just doesn't work.' Previn said, 'It's hard not to make accents until the fourth bar', and Silverstein said, 'Stress the first beat, and separate it from the second note.' They started the scherzo again, and Silverstein stopped and laughed and said, 'It's easier for me to be with the piano than the piano to be with me' – a role reversal that caused Previn to say, 'Well, it shouldn't be.'

The last movement, like the Franck's second movement, begins with the violin playing on the G-string, but with the Brahms the melody is a warm, rich cantabile – in contrast to the somewhat stormy Franck. In the development, Silverstein played a repeated phrase the second time like a fragile echo, and Previn stopped. He said, 'You do something *so* nice there that I want to do it again.' It was the kind of subtlety in superb musicianship that is breathtaking. Then the piano had the melody, threaded through light chords. It takes great skill to play rich Brahms chords lightly. The violin had accompanying counterpoint. Previn stopped and said, 'This. I love this phrase so much' – he repeated the passage. 'It comes out of nowhere.'

Silverstein said, 'You know what it comes out of. It comes out of the slow movement of the "Jupiter" Symphony.'

Previn said, 'Oh, come *on.*'

Silverstein said, 'Yes – sure. The syncopated changes.' He played a passage from the Mozart symphony, exaggerating the syncopation. 'You know that place? Brahms wrote about that in a letter to Joachim. He was wildly enamoured of the slow movement of the "Jupiter".' (One of Brahms's most often quoted maxims was 'If we cannot write as beautifully as Mozart and Haydn, let us at least write as purely.')

Previn smiled and said, 'If only Mozart had had a piano with a pedal.' Then he said, 'Ah. Listen, Joey. Here' – he backtracked to another thicket of chords containing the melody. 'Don't rush me there.' Silverstein said, 'Did I? I didn't mean to', and Previn said, 'On the other hand, *here* I simply came unglued.'

Silverstein said, 'Let's go back and do it again. I don't want to rush you', and Previn said, 'Nor do I want to come unglued.'

They picked up where they had left off, and played to the end – the violin finishing with a rich double-stop melody against four-octave arpeggiated chords in the piano, and then two final chords.

Previn said, 'That's much better. I think I know what I'm doing now. Those six-four chords. Those guys. Right out of Strauss, and beyond.' He played the chord transpositions that had pleased him so much – Silverstein was cheering him on with 'Yeah's – and sang the theme. 'And get this' – he continued. He was speechless. Silverstein said, 'I know. He keeps feeding it to you, and

154

then he says, "And by the way. . ." '

Previn said, 'I have no history of this piece, Joey, so I'm just feeling my way.' He stood up and stretched. He bummed a cigarette from Silverstein and said, 'I'd like to have at least a brief rehearsal onstage.' They agreed to meet again the following day, and outside Heather was waiting to drive Previn home. He was so unhappy about how the Brahms had gone – *his* part – that later, in the evening, he called Silverstein to apologise for his playing, to Silverstein's surprise. It's possible that with any other composer Previn would not have felt inadequate first time around. He has said of Brahms, in general, 'There is always a beautiful melody *struggling* to get out.'

CHAPTER 4

Previn met with the seminar conductors at one o'clock on Thursday afternoon at Seranak to work with several of them as, one by one, they conducted a piece of his or her choice, conducting the two pianos. Tanglewood was enjoying a driving rain that now and then became a deluge – a blessed relief from the prolonged heat wave. The rain washed the leaves until they glistened and gave sweet sustenance to the blossoming plants that proliferate all over the Berkshires every summer.

Some fifteen-odd conductors from as many different states and nations gathered shortly before one in the same room where Previn had talked to the students in 1980. The dress was casual, and, because the day was chilly, there was a preponderance of turtlenecks – many conductors' favourite rehearsal dress. Previn had on a checked red-and-white long-sleeved shirt and jeans. Gustav Meier was seated at the front of the room, and toward the rear several students were gathered around Previn, talking to him.

Promptly at one, Previn took a seat next to Meier, and the students sat on the grey folding chairs, pulled up to be close to the action. They all had piles of scores next to their chairs; a great deal of repertoire would be covered during the summer. If love of music, and a deep commitment to it, were a saleable commodity, everyone in the room would be wealthy. But wealth of another kind was palpable. At the front of the room, the two pianos were placed next to each other, keyboards facing the students, at diagonals, so the two pianists – who were already in place – could see each other.

Also in place, standing between and behind the pianos and facing the class, was the first conductor, Naohiro

Totsuka. Mr Totsuka had a string of prizes and a lot of conducting experience in Japan. A slight, quiet man, he had an interpreter by his side, to help out. His English was minimal. He had chosen to conduct the last movement of the Beethoven Seventh Symphony. The symphony was composed in 1812, when Beethoven was in a comparatively happy frame of mind, for him, and at the height of his powers. Most descriptions of the last movement include the word 'bacchanalian', and some call it 'a tremendous dance'. It is filled with cosmic crescendos and insidious, insistent rhythms. At its first rehearsal, the string players at first refused to even attempt it, pronouncing it unplayable. The conductor was Beethoven, and he persuaded them to take the chance. The two pianists would get some workout.

Totsuka had a presence, a command as he conducted. The movement opens with two eight-bar phrases, each repeated, and its tempo marking is allegro con brio – fast. Previn stopped him. 'When you have the rests, in the second ending' – he sang the phrase – 'you don't have to give them both beats. The tempo stays absolute. It's difficult to *lose* it. And after the repeated phrase you must give them an upbeat in the same tempo.'

Totsuka resumed conducting; the two pianos understandably sounded even more percussive than that instrument can.

Previn stopped him. 'Now, when you got to this point' – he showed him his score – 'it got a little slower. On purpose?' Laughter. 'It would not be a bad idea, because it's been *very* fast. The tempo is fine, if that's your choice, but you might want to start just a little bit under tempo. And another thing. After the sforzando, you gesture for a crescendo. Do you really want a crescendo?' A nod, 'Yes.'

Previn said, 'Do you have a reason?'

The interpreter explained that Totsuka just wanted the sound sustained through the end of the bar.

Previn said, 'Ah. You want them to hang on. That's different. With your direction, you'll get a loud scratch from the strings – a squawk, with a crescendo on top of a sforzando. And you don't want that, because you're already fortissimo, and it's too much. But you're right to want them to hang on to the sound.' He spoke to the class. 'Let me ask you something. Do you all have scores? Yes? At letter D. You have the winds and the brass together. What would you tell them? How would you balance it? The horns are going to be *very* loud. What should you tell them so you don't have a big mess in those four bars?' He paused, and then said, 'Look, it's silly to make a quizz out of this. The horns have the melody. Let them play fortissimo up to that point, then drop down, so that the woodwind melody can be heard. Those open E octaves in the horns don't mean a lot – they're just filler. Speaking generally, it's a pretty *pounding* rhythm in this movement anyway, and especially at that tempo. It's good, as long as they're together.' Laughter. 'I would say this to you: this piece is full of accents. If you have a lot of people playing fortissimo plus accents, it's going to be a little crazy. You're going to hear a *tremendous* racket. What you really want to do, in a piece like this, with so many accents, instead of playing the accents louder make the notes around them a little softer. It will give you the same effect, still be very loud, and the accents will feel like accents instead of the end of the world.' Laughter.

Totsuka resumed conducting and finished the movement without interruption. As the end approached, momentum built, Beethoven unleashed all the orchestral forces, and the two pianos sounded more like twelve. At the conclusion, the players and Totsuka were applauded.

Previn said, 'It's very good. But I think you beat too much, because at the end of this movement the tiredest one of them all is going to be you, and it should be the other way around.' Laughter. 'You're going to be *exhausted*. Once a piece like this gets rolling, it doesn't need much from you. Also, some of the cues you give, you do it *as* it happens, at the same moment. It's too late. In other words, if someone comes in on one, and you *give* them one, that's not going to help him. If he wants to breathe, if he's unsure, you're not going to help him. You have to cue him in advance – either by a look or a specific pick-up. But you can't give a cue as it happens. It's too late.

'You have a very nice idea. During all this you were concentrating on that pattern' – he sang a repeated two-tone phrase, half-tone intervals, Western music's closest interval, called 'false relations', which hits the nerve ends when relentlessly, insistently repeated – 'which is wonderful. That's where the "threatening" is – the extraordinary sense of danger that goes on in this piece. But you can get that started a little earlier. I have a theory, which is just an opinion, that when you have a very *long* crescendo that goes on for a long time, if you start it at the bottom end of the orchestra a little earlier than upstairs it will really work wonders. You'll find a kind of organic growth coming out. Instead of just the tune or the decoration getting louder, you'll feel the thing it's sitting on getting louder. Very often, I will delay a printed crescendo in the higher register until I make it apparent that it's *going* to happen by strengthening lower strings, lower winds.'

Previn looked at the score again, and said, 'Explain something to me. Here, at the very end, you make repeated accents. Why?' The interpreter explained. Previn said, 'Oh, the timpani. Well, once – yes. But not every time. He won't need it. Probably he won't even be looking at you.' Laughter. 'I mean, he's pretty busy. And I think you'll confuse him, because he'll think he put the accent on the wrong place. Generally speaking, in a piece like this, when you get it going, leave it alone a little. Also – it's impossible with pianos – when it gets softer in the orchestra there is a way of making it seem slower without being slower, by making it more graceful.' He sang the theme liltingly. In the pianos' performance it had sounded thundering. 'The way you were beating it, that forte in the winds was *whack*!' He clapped his hands. 'It's just a little spray. And if you beat all that' – he sang it heavy, thunderous – 'it's going to be simply hysterical. There *are* moments of relaxation in this piece. Let them happen. Also, when you have a sforzando followed by a fortissimo, which do you think is louder?' The class said, 'Fortissimo', nearly in unison.

Previn said to Totsuka, 'The way you were conducting it, I wasn't sure. One thing you'll find when you stand in front of an orchestra – not the Boston – with crescendos, *invariably* they start too soon. Players see a twenty-bar crescendo – especially string players – and within five bars they've already reached what you want from them after twenty bars. So you have to be careful in your gestures not to encourage them right away. Make them aware of it, but do this to them' – he made a broad gesture – 'and Holy Moses. There's no stopping them. In this movement, it should be wildest on the last page, and not before. But it was very, very good. Very fine.' Prolonged, loud applause.

Kay Roberts, a trim, very attractive light-skinned black, hair held back in a knot, black slacks, black turtleneck under a white shirt open at the throat, took Totsuka's place. Previn asked her what she would like to do. She said, 'The second movement.'

Previn said, 'Of this piece?' She looked confused and repeated 'Of this piece?'

Previn said, 'I'm asking, not saying. I know a couple more.' Laughter.

Miss Roberts said, 'The same piece.'

The second movement begins in A-minor, with a sustained chord in the winds and brass. The tempo, allegretto, and Beethoven's nearly sunny mood keep the slow movement from being funereal. The melodies are simple, and so natural they seem to come from the human experience at its most serene. It moves into A-major, and it's as if Beethoven were saying, 'Life goes on.' At its first performance, the audience demanded, and got, a repeat of the movement. In Beethoven's day, some conductors substituted the movement for the Eighth Symphony's slow movement, because they liked it so much.

160

Miss Roberts was well into the theme when Previn stopped her. 'When you do the eighth notes [quavers]' – he sang the phrase – 'it gets slower. If you mean that, then that's called "interpretation", and I won't argue. If you don't mean it, it's wrong.' Soft laughter.

Miss Roberts said, 'I *mean* it.' Loud laughter from the class, and Previn laughed, too.

She continued to conduct, and Previn said, 'When you want them to do the pianissimo, let them know in the rest before – just with a look. Don't let them know as they play. It's too late. And I'm not convinced that the second beat of the bar, with the two eighth notes, is the same tempo as the downbeat. You're getting slower.' He sang the phrase. 'It should be like dripping water. I don't think your colleagues at the piano *know* what you want. This is one of those pieces where you can really leave it the hell alone. Do it once more.'

He stopped her again. 'I know Mr Ozawa spends time on absolutely technical things, and I wasn't here this year when Lenny worked with you, but I'm sure it was the reverse of that – what the music is about. [Indeed. Ozawa worked with one conductor on baton technique, comparing the movement of the wrist with the pitch of a baseball, and Bernstein, reclining in a chair, said to another conductor, 'Give me brilliance! Brilliance!' and 'Lead us into paradise!'] Obviously, conducting the phrase is more important than conducting the beat. But in the meantime you have to be able to conduct technically so that which you mean is able to come out. So both things are equally valid.'

She started again, and after eight bars she stopped, laughed, and apologised. It was faster than she had intended.

Previn said, 'Actually, I like that tempo. After all, it's an allegretto. I think you'll find this is a very *long* movement if you take it too slow.' Laughter.

She proceeded into the movement, and the development of the theme. Previn stopped her. He said, 'I think sometimes, in your determination not to be just a metronome, you become too much the opposite of one. You're interfering with things. For instance, when the seconds have' – he sang a phrase the way he felt it should be, subtle leading, and then what she had conducted, bold, important – 'it's not very interesting without the next bar. You have to think, "Where is it going?" Your way, there's no place left to go. It's going to the E. And the fact that it's a nice motion, and you want it brought out, *that* you can tell them. Also – this is the time to be picky, is it not?'

Miss Roberts said, 'Absolutely.'

Previn said, 'When there is a rest, you very rarely make it the same tempo as the beat before or after. You get suckered into doing it either faster or slower. Very often – not in this piece – as you all know, sometimes the rest has to be the loudest part of the bar. When nobody's playing. Also, here, you should be aware that before the winds join in on this, it should already have an extremely rich stringy sound. Don't let all this beginning just be an introduction to the winds.'

Miss Roberts said, 'I *thought* of it as an introduction.'

Previn said, 'Well, this piece can be interpreted a million ways, but by the time the firsts are piu forte, the strings can really *sing*. It's extremely beautiful. And then, when the winds come in, it's a completely different game anyway. So let the strings have their say at the beginning. And you must be careful.' He sang the leading phrase. 'The listener expects the last note of the phrase to be forte. It's a pianissimo, without a break. Part of Beethoven's genius eccentricity is the eccentricity of dynamic extremes. If he puts a pianissimo at the least logical place, or a fortissimo, *that's* where you do it. Don't ever let people cheat because it's more comfortable.'

She continued, and he stopped her. 'When the firsts come in, they have a long series of Es, and then by virtue of a single F-sharp they have a long series of Gs, in which case you were quite right to bring out the tune in the seconds. When, at the end of that phrase, the firsts have a

162

counter melody, then they suddenly have a right to produce more sound, and if it is equal with the seconds it will be very beautiful. When they have just repeated notes, fine. Then they're just an accompaniment. But when they come in with an actual tune, don't have them play so thinly, just because the seconds have the actual thematic material.'

She said, 'I know. It's counterpoint.'

She continued to the beginning of the A-major section, and he said, 'This is a piece where you don't really want a lot of rubatos. But, on the other hand, what you want even less, in a way, is bar-by-bar sledge-hammering. This is a great piece – especially when you get to the fortissimo and the winds are in. You can really conduct the phrase. No orchestra is going to need a one-two beat that big, that defined, on each bar line. It's such a *sensational* tune. Conduct that, and where you think it ought to go, and don't worry so much.'

She resumed conducting and again he stopped her. 'I have to ask you something. Is it natural for you to close your eyes? With all *phenomenal* admiration due Mr von Karajan' – laughter – 'I've never understood how he can conduct with his eyes closed. I don't mean this as a put-down, but when you do that musicians will think you're overcome with it all, and they're not going to look at you anymore, or they'll think you don't know what you're doing, which, of course, is even worse. You don't have to fix everybody with a piercing glance, but don't go to sleep.' She laughed and said, 'I won't', and the class laughed, too.

When the movement shifted to A-major, the mood was sunnier, and when she was well into that section Previn stopped her. 'You have been lulled into a serious case of the A-majors there.' Laughter. 'He *does* keep the rhythm going, and you did not start at the tempo you're conducting now. Because it's so *pretty* it's perfectly fair to relax it, but I think by now it's getting close to tedious.' Laughter. 'So move it. If you want the whole piece that slow, again, that's up to you. But since you didn't start anywhere near this tempo, I think it's getting dangerous.'

She continued until he interrupted again. 'Look. If you were to sing some of these phrases, you would know a little bit more where they're going. Surely' – he showed her a place in his score; she was conducting from memory – 'this would not be exactly the same as what precedes it. It's always *going* someplace. Look where it is, where it's going, and whether the next phrase is a continuation, a repeat, or what. Then you can concentrate on conducting the phrase. You're still too much worried about the accompaniment. It will take care of itself.'

Miss Roberts laughed and said, 'I hope so', and he said, 'But you'll find *out*. You can always go back to nailing somebody with a quick beat if things aren't together. But before you can conduct the phrase, you've got to work out where it is and what it's doing and why it's there.'

She continued, and came to a four-octave semiquaver descending scale passed from winds to violins to violas to cellos and basses, ending with two fortissimo quavers. He stopped her. 'There you want to be careful. Don't let those two eighth notes sound like the end of the piece.' He slammed the piano with his fist and said, 'Bam. Bam. Applause.' Laughter. 'It's not stopping there. It goes on.'

She repeated the passage and successfully negotiated the descending scale and the two quavers leading into the dolce theme in the woodwinds.

Previn stopped her and asked, 'What's your instrument?'

Miss Roberts said, 'Violin.'

'Ah. Well, try to listen to, let's say, a good singer doing a Schubert song, and watch where she has to breathe, and watch where the melody has to breathe. I think that you are not allowing the tunes in your head, or here, to breathe. You've learned what's in each bar perfectly, but it doesn't have an organic flow – it should *get* somewhere. You're too concerned about the mechanics of keeping people together. You'd be surprised how it all falls into place. They'll straighten that out anyway. Even for those

164

of us who aren't good enough, they'll very often straighten it out. But those who have a theme, a tune, a fragment, a breath – they have to know where it's coming from. And if you don't have that – whether in your face, in your eyes, in your *breathing* – they won't know what you want.'

Miss Roberts said, 'I'm *trying* to make it visible.'

Previn said, ' "Visible" is something you have to get into your head first. You have to think about it, and work it out.' He had told her at a previous session that she was not assertive enough – that she must have an attitude toward an orchestra of 'I'm the conductor here, and if you don't like it, screw you.' Now he said, 'But you're much more assertive than you were last time, and that's good.' The class applauded, and she returned to her seat.

The class took a ten-minute break, and then Previn helped a third conductor through part of the first movement of the Beethoven, a fourth student with the opening section of Tchaikovsky's *Romeo and Juliet*, and then he addressed the students: 'I think basically what it comes down to is that a lot of you seem to be concerned with the *way* you are doing something, instead of primarily what it is you want to *hear*. I studied with Monteux, and he used to say to us, "*Any*thing is fair." You can do the most eccentric, the most offbeat things in the world *if* they elicit that which you have in your head and in your soul that you want to hear. And I think some of you – forgive me – have it the other way around. I think you've figured out how to do something, and that that will produce the desired result. You have to know what the desired result is, and suit the action to that.'

The class applauded. Previn had become so involved with the musicians that no one could set a watch by him today. They were all twenty minutes late for the next appointment, including Previn, who raced down the hill to a studio on the Tanglewood grounds, where he coached two pianists who were working on the two-piano version of the Rachmaninoff 'Symphonic Dances', which Previn had recorded with Vladimir Ashkenazy.

165

At season's end, Previn was presented with a matted, framed photograph of himself conducting the student orchestra. The mat held the signatures of all the faculty members, the members of the orchestra, the conducting students, and the two pianists. Printed in blue edged with gold letters was the message 'To André Previn, with Gratitude From the Fellows of the Berkshire Music Center – 1983.' The last time such a gesture was made at Tanglewood was in 1944, for Serge Koussevitzky.

Part IV

CHAPTER 1

Previn likes to begin a new season with an exciting programme – an 'unimpeachable programme' – to please the audience and to stimulate subscription sales. In September of 1983, he opened the season with a prodigy violinist – the American-born, Korean, thirteen-year-old Eunice Lee. Two years earlier, Previn had been the guest conductor of the Chicago Symphony, and that orchestra's co-leader, Samuel Magad, who also teaches, invited Previn to hear his best pupil, Eunice Lee. When Previn heard Eunice play, he was so impressed that he asked, on the spot, if she would come to Pittsburgh to play with his orchestra. She told him that she had promised 'Mr Solti' that she would play with the Chicago Symphony first, but she would very much like to play for Previn in Pittsburgh after that. Eunice's date with the Chicago was cancelled because of an orchestra strike, so she made her official American début with a major orchestra in Pittsburgh, on 9 September.

Previn said, 'I hadn't heard her in two years, and I began to worry: maybe she isn't as good as I thought she was. Maybe she hasn't progressed in two years. If this isn't successful, *everyone* – management, orchestra, public – will land on me.' He scheduled a piano rehearsal with Eunice on Monday, and she was even better than he could possibly have anticipated. She had chosen for her début the Paganini Concerto No. 1, because it is a fireworks' display of technique. Previn was surprised. He said, 'Even successful concert violinists blow more than a few notes in that concerto.' It is riddled with treacherous fast harmonic scales, double-stop harmonic passages, fingered octaves and runs in tenths. Paganini composed

169

the piece to show off his own technique; *none* of his colleagues could play it.

Photographs of Eunice during the first orchestra rehearsal, wearing shorts and blouse and sandals, her long black hair pulled back in a ponytail, show her digging into the music, confident and poised and even aggressive. Some of the orchestra members are grinning with pleasure; some look thunderstruck. If one shut one's eyes, it would be impossible to believe that a child was producing that full, gutsy, rich tone, playing those incredibly difficult passages so effortlessly and flawlessly. After the first performance, in which Eunice was dressed in a flounced full-skirted white dress and white silk slippers that made her look like a beautiful fairy princess, the audience in Heinz Hall leaped up, as one, and applauded and shouted 'Bravo!' Previn kissed her on the cheek, and when a bouquet of roses was presented to her she drew one from the bunch, handed it to Previn, and returned the kiss, causing him to comment later, 'She doesn't have much more to learn.'

All Friday night, Previn lay awake – partly from excitement and partly from worry. Could she possibly do it again on Saturday night? And Sunday afternoon? Her playing had moved him in so many ways. When he wasn't looking at her, he completely forgot she was a child; when he looked at her his eyes filled with tears. She deeply touched Previn in the two areas where he is most touchable: youth and music. The combination nearly bowled him over.

At each concert, Eunice's mother walked with her daughter to the stage door and gave her a big hug. Before going onstage for the Sunday-afternoon concert, Previn, his hand resting on Eunice's shoulder, said, 'Well, what do you want to play this time? The Paganini again? Or something else?' The critics said that the date of Eunice's début should go down in history, along with those of Heifetz and Menuhin. The reviews, plus word of mouth, drew throngs of people to the hall who hoped to buy

170

tickets. Four abreast, they were in a line that stretched halfway around the block all day Saturday and Sunday until concert-time. One audience member was heard to say, 'When you hear this, you *have* to believe in God', and another said, 'It makes you believe in reincarnation.' Anne Martindale Williams, the principal cellist, introduced herself to Eunice after the first rehearsal, and Eunice told her that she had always wanted to play the cello – that it was her favourite instrument. Mrs Williams clasped Eunice's hand in both of hers and said, 'Oh, thank you for *not*!'

Previn appeared before the Executive Committee of the Board of Directors the following week, to give them a progress report, and to tell the members about things that bothered him, things that needed doing. He told them that his main concern was that the orchestra was being made to feel second-rate, demeaned, humiliated – 'the conditions of where they play in the summer, and a million other things, and a kind of nickel-and-dime theory that when there is a way to do them out of five dollars apiece it's taken. That has *got* to stop, because they are artists. They are musically so worthy, and so ready to compete with even the Boston and the Chicago.' Previn was gathering steam. He said, 'Look. There are fifteen orchestras in the world that mean anything. Figuring a hundred people per orchestra, that's fifteen hundred people who make the world's greatest music. That's very few in terms of the population of the world. You can't *treat* them like factory workers. They're very special people.'

Previn then left the meeting. He had to rehearse the orchestra, and also, he said, whatever else they talked about was none of his business. After he left the room (it was later reported to him by a committee member) the orchestra's managing director, Marshall Turkin, apologised for Previn's speech – said that it was out of line, and that he didn't know what he was talking about. He said, 'I've been in the music business for years. Believe me, I know about musicians.'

Previn had been promised a chamber-music series for

171

the 1983–84 season. He'd been asking for one ever since he had come to Pittsburgh. He said, 'All good orchestras have them. The Vienna, the Chicago, the Berlin. It's a wonderful opportunity for all the members of the orchestra to lose their invisibility, be heard, show how good they are, and play with visiting soloists, who all like to play in such series. There are so many good players in the orchestra. They *deserve* exposure.'

After the board meeting, Turkin told Previn that he had been wrong about the orchestra's having a chamber-music series this season – that for monetary reasons it would have to be postponed a year. Previn reported to me that his response was ' "It's too late, I've already announced it, and so many orchestra members want to be involved in it that if I cancel it now there will be an insurrection." Marshall *always* has trouble with words. His response would be *hilarious* if it weren't so pathetic. He said, "A resurrection! Well, if there's going to be a resurrection, obviously you can't cancel now. We'll find the money somehow." '

Previn then went to the orchestra and said, 'We're going to have a chamber-music series, starting in February. Those of you who are interested, come see me after the rehearsal.' Almost seventy came to see him.

Managing directors are an integral part of any orchestra, and they are so scarce that in 1980 Previn told me that if the board had to choose between him and Turkin they would pick Turkin without hesitation. He was nearly invisible the times I went to Pittsburgh; he stayed in his aerie on the top, fifth floor of Heinz Hall, and had as little as possible to do with the musicians. If musicians' complaints reached the board, Turkin, according to Previn, would say, 'What do you care what *they* think?' The board liked Turkin, Previn felt, because he was such a good bookkeeper. Previn had been accustomed to fighting for every single thing he wanted for his orchestra, but there were times when Turkin – like the catalyst Hollywood producer who caused Previn to flee Hollywood because he moved his lips when he read – could have got Previn to be voluntarily shot from a cannon to get out of Pittsburgh and away from Turkin, if it weren't for the orchestra Previn loved. Turkin sometimes seemed to be a thorn-in-the-flesh, salt-in-the-wound, fingernail-on-a-blackboard to Previn. But Previn always said he could get along with him, that he could get along with anybody. (He cites as an example a leader with the LSO. He says, 'We bickered constantly, and one day the managing director told me, "You'll be happy to hear we fired the concertmaster", and I said, "Why, for Chrissake?" and he said, "You two fight all the time", and I said, "So what? That has nothing to do with anything. He's a terrific concertmaster." ') Discretion is not second but first nature to Previn, and with the exception of one or two close friends, he concealed his dislike of Turkin. He had lunch with him often to discuss orchestra business, and when I first came to Pittsburgh he praised Turkin to me as being valuable when it came to programming – adroit at picking the perfect piece to balance a programme. To his friends he groaned. One of them greeted him on a Tuesday with 'How are you?' Previn said, 'How the hell do you think I am? I just spent the morning with Marshall, and Reagan was elected.'

In the fall of 1983, Previn revealed a few things about Turkin that bothered him. He had a few minutes free before a rehearsal was to begin. He said, 'It isn't that I dislike Marshall so much as I fail to understand him. I don't understand the way he acts, nor do I understand the way he reacts. I don't understand his attitude toward the musicians, or his attitude toward his work, and the thing that makes it hopeless, and this is really important, is that he doesn't understand *that*. Even if you resurrected Freud and had a daily depth analysis, at the end Marshall would still say, "I don't know what you're talking about." He's too old to change. His personality is forever ingrained. Years ago, I once said to him, "Marshall, you are having some trouble with the orchestra because you are, by nature, so secretive, and the orchestra is forced to read in the newspapers what they're doing, where they're going, whose coming, all their plans, whether local, national, or international. They hear about things *after* plans are completed. Marshall said, "They're not supposed to know." And I said, "But they're the ones who have to do the playing. There's a certain percentage of that orchestra that does not believe you. They don't trust you. Honestly, it would be so easy to fix. If there are plans for us to go on a tour to such-and-such, *tell* them. They would love to hear that they are in demand, that people want to hear them all over the world." He said, "But what happens if it doesn't pan out?" I said, "You just say, 'I'm terribly sorry that one didn't pan out, but we have seventeen other things in the fire.' " He said, "I don't believe you", and I said, "You don't believe what *part* of it?" "I don't believe the orchestra doesn't trust me or doesn't like me. It's out of the question. They don't think about those things, except a few agitators and troublemakers." '

In 1982, Previn began conducting concerts in a sleeveless black tunic over a white shirt, open at the throat, and black trousers. He rationalised that Seiji Ozawa dressed comfortably when he conducted, and so did Karajan. The first time he appeared onstage in the outfit, the orchestra members giggled. Pittsburgh was reportedly enraged – especially some board members. He steadfastly refused or wiggled out of their dinner invitations, and now he was dressing in a manner that some board members claimed would be a bad influence on their children. Previn had been plagued by a painful arthritic condition in both feet for some time – only drastic surgery would correct the problem – and he was unyielding. He felt entitled to *some* comfort when he worked.

CHAPTER 2

In October, in London, Previn recorded the six ninety-minute programmes on the development of the symphony with the Royal Philharmonic Orchestra. There was instant rapport between the conductor and the orchestra, an immediate love affair, according to Heather, who sat in on the sessions. Previn pronounced the orchestra in pristine shape. He said it was the first time he'd worked with them on such a serious basis, though it was the RPO that was the orchestra for the television performance of *Every Good Boy Deserves Favour*.

Previn and Bert Chapple both did research for information about the composers and their works, which would be used as examples of the symphony's development. Their combined information was put on five-by-eight cards, and during the actual filming Previn, as is his custom, discarded the cards and spoke extemporaneously.

The programmes were co-produced by Arts International Limited and the BBC, and described in a colour brochure published for the information of sponsors:

PROGRAMME ONE: Haydn and Mozart. Haydn's Symphony No. 87 and Mozart's Symphony No. 39. 'The symphonies of Haydn and Mozart represent a landmark in the history of Western music. Living at a time when the composer was fast making the transition from being an individual with a personal and committed voice, Haydn and Mozart laid firm foundations for a rich form of musical expression that finds its most magnificent and powerful expression in that strange phenomenon called the "symphony". They wrote over one hundred and fifty symphonies between them and their influence has had a lasting effect on later symphonic forms and

175

styles, and on the development of the symphony orchestra.'

PROGRAMME TWO: Beethoven. Excerpts from Beethoven's Symphony No. 5 and a performance of the Symphony No. 7. 'Most securely established of all orchestral music, the symphonies of Beethoven were often greeted by his contemporaries with as much amazement as respect. Weber, composer of *Der Freischütz*, declared that "on the strength of his Seventh Symphony Beethoven should be locked away in a madhouse". Others declared that Beethoven must clearly have been drunk to compose such absurd and untamed music. This programme demonstrates how Beethoven brought an unprecedented power and dynamism to the orchestra and questions how far he was affected by the idealism of the French Revolution and by the personal reality of his incurable deafness.'

PROGRAMME THREE: Berlioz's 'Symphonie Fantastique'. 'In Paris on 11 September 1982, the French composer Hector Berlioz fell madly in love with an Irish actress, Harriet Smithson. The intensity of his infatuation and the twists and turns of their relationship became inextricably tangled with a symphony he was to compose, a composition that broke new ground with the lavish virtuosity of its orchestration. Berlioz's "Symphonie Fantastique" is acclaimed as one of the most extraordinary and truly original works ever written.'

PROGRAMME FOUR: Brahms's Symphony No. 4. 'André Previn's introduction to Brahms's Fourth Symphony gives an understanding of why composers persistently take up the challenge of writing works of symphonic stature. Unlike other musical expressions a symphony cannot be faked. In an opera or ballet there is a story, scenery, costumes and effects to distract an audience. In a concerto there is always the charisma of the soloist, or the sheer brilliance of the playing to mask flaws in the

176

composition. But with a symphony the work is judged only on the quality of the composer's writing and his ability to develop his musical ideas.'

PROGRAMME FIVE: Tchaikovsky's Symphony No. 6 (the 'Pathétique'). 'For years Tchaikovsky has been frowned on by the musical establishment, for the most illogical of reasons – because he is a truly popular composer. His music is direct in its appeal, tuneful and highly emotional. André Previn looks at why Tchaikovsky's music holds such magic and why an audience responds to it time and time again. The "Pathétique" Symphony is Tchaikovsky's last composition, first performed barely a week before his mysterious and tragic death.'

PROGRAMME SIX: Shostakovich's Symphony No. 5. 'In the final programme of this series André Previn talks about modern symphonic works and the new sophisticated language of musical expression. Shostakovich encountered the peril of being an experimental composer living under Stalin's régime at a time when "difficult" composers incurred official displeasure and were known to disappear overnight. Certain that he would be arrested he kept a small suitcase packed and ready, but Stalin was too clever to eliminate Shostakovich. Yet when Shostakovich produced his Fifth Symphony music undoubtedly triumphed over politics.'

The programmes would offer the viewer much more information than the bare-bones outline. Previn was pleased with the format. He said that the 'Previn and the Pittsburgh's were concerts with a little talk tacked on. In these ninety-minute broadcasts there would be ample time for explanation and amplification and something Previn can't stay away from (unless it's inappropriate): humour.

Toward the end of the recording sessions, Previn moved Heather and the children to a hotel in London. The baby was due, and he wisely wanted his wife to be near the hospital. On Sunday, 28 October, a day off from rehearsing and recording, Lukas Alexander Previn was born. Previn told the orchestra members about the baby the next morning, in the studio, and one RPO musician pronounced Lukas's timing 'the zenith of professionalism'. Previn, who had always said that his children should do in life whatever made them happy, told the orchestra members, 'You should see his hands! Cellist's hands!'

In December, when Previn got back to Surrey, he checked into a London hospital and had foot surgery. The pain was worse than he'd anticipated – but not the worst he'd ever experienced. He said to a friend, 'Don't forget all those provincial orchestras I conducted.' Heather visited him daily, bringing Lukas along; for the most part Previn, who averages five hours' sleep a night, slept. After ten days, he went home to recuperate, and he directed the trimming of the Christmas tree from an easy chair. Before Christmas, Norman Lebrecht, of the London *Times*, came to Surrey to interview Previn. In an article headed, 'Four Ages of a Musician for All Seasons', Lebrecht had these things to say:

It is entirely characteristic of André Previn that he should have started work as music director of the Royal Philharmonic Orchestra almost two years ahead of his official installation in June 1985. Whatever else may have changed (and much has) in the four years since he ceased to be a fixture in London's musical firmament, Previn's enthusiasm and appetite for work remain insatiable.

For four months of each year he is committed to the Pittsburgh Symphony Orchestra, whose music director he has been since 1976. The rest of the time he flits about guest-conducting the world's major orchestras in Berlin, Vienna, Amsterdam, London, Boston, Chicago, Philadelphia, and New York. In addition he goes on chamber music tours with the principals of the Vienna Philharmonic, records two LPs every three months (he has

178

contracts to fulfil with both EMI and Philips), composes and writes (his *Guide to Music* is published this month by Macmillan). He also makes television programmes and commercials. 'I don't know how not to work so hard,' he says flatly. 'I'm crazy about my profession. When somebody offers me two weeks in Amsterdam or Boston, before I know what I've said, I've said "yes." ' . . .

On television, his versatility is unique among musicians, surpassing the raw passion of Bernstein's pioneering programmes with a sophisticated array of devices calculated to lure the least musical of viewers. Previn is at home on television, more so perhaps than anywhere else. . .

The Previn who has set out to recapture a dominant position in musical London is no longer the glib, flip pixie who galvanised it in the early 1970s. Previn is on the threshold of his fourth period.

The first, now almost a childish irrelevance, was the Hollywood era as jazz pianist, film composer and Oscar accumulator. The second saw his rise to musical respectability via Houston and the LSO.

In the third, his Pittsburgh leadership and Public Broadcasting Service programmes won him acceptability in the US. The fourth period, his re-entry into a now-troubled London music arena, could well determine the conclusive verdict of history on this meteoric performer. . . The third period has also brought greater maturity as a conductor. His musical relationship with the Pittsburgh added administrative experience to his musical authority. As Music Director (at the LSO he was merely Principal Conductor), he is responsible for everything from hiring and firing players to programming the children's concerts. He will undertake similar responsibilities at the RPO and, he believes, it is no coincidence that the LSO has swiftly upgraded Claudio Abbado's status to Music Director.

'When I came to work here in 1968,' he reflects, 'it was absolutely undeniable that London was the greatest musical centre in the world. That position is much shakier now – for reasons of inflation, recession, the decline of audiences and the record industry. It used to be taken for granted that a good programme, or soloist, or conductor, would fill the Festival Hall. That is no longer the case.'. . .

He has persisted with the advancement of British music that he began in London. It was Previn, more than any other, who restored Vaughan Williams and Walton to general circulation – and has given the US premiere of Tippett's Triple Concerto, as well as works by John McCabe, Oliver Knussen, and Nicholas Maw. . .

One of the highlights of his career was to take Britten and Walton to Russia with the LSO in 1970. 'They were about as friendly as Britten and Walton were going to be,' he laughs, 'but I was just pleased to be in the same room. Sir William was thrilled with the screaming ovation – about twenty minutes of it – that his First Symphony got in Moscow.' Previn treasures a photograph of himself and Walton in full concert dress clutching cans of beer as Russian officialdom toasted them in vodka.

On the Soviet tour, Previn established his own reputation as an outstanding interpreter of Russian music. In the meantime, however, since collaborating with Tom Stoppard on *Every Good Boy Deserves Favour*, a musical set in a Soviet psychiatric hospital, he is no longer welcome in the Soviet Union. An attempt last year to return with an American television network to cover the International Tchaikovsky Competition was discreetly but efficiently blocked. It was just after the Barbican revival of *EGBDF* opened in Vienna he found himself unable to enter East Germany to record the Brahms *Requiem* in Dresden. 'I had a very kind letter from the orchestra, saying how sorry they were.'

His forthcoming compositions are less controversial. There is a long-promised piano concerto for Vladimir

Ashkenazy which he expects to complete by next summer, and an orchestral piece commissioned by the Vienna Philharmonic Orchestra for the 1985 Salzburg Festival.

Despite the pedigree of his clients, Previn makes no undue claims for himself as composer or conductor. He is acutely aware of his own limitations and of market realities, refusing for example to consider the possibility of recording a Beethoven cycle, the conductor's ultimate accolade. 'If someone goes into a record shop and asks for the "Eroica", and he is then given a list of everyone since Nikisch who recorded it, why wouldn't he pick some gigantic interpretation? No, I never think of records as a vanity. I'd like them to have some validity and I'd like them to sell enough so that the company isn't sorry they were made.' In fact his sales record is such that he has made more recordings than any but three or four other conductors in the history of the gramophone [Previn has won seven Edison awards]. . .

For a man who overextends himself so consistently, Previn has reduced his failure rate to a barely perceptible minimum. He no longer has to fly by the seat of his pants, learning music as he conducts it. The whizzkid is still whirling, but a purpose and direction may be discerned as he prepares his return to London.

In January, Previn brought Heather and the baby to Pittsburgh, where he would conduct three weekends of concerts before taking the orchestra to Hong Kong for an eight-day Arts Festival. Heather had hoped to go, too, but Lukas's paediatrician was against it. On Tuesday morning, the day of the first rehearsal, Previn announced from the podium that there was someone he wanted the musicians to meet. He left the stage and returned, carrying Lukas in his arms. Lukas waved his arms happily, which tickled Previn and made the orchestra members laugh. (Previn was still very uncomfortable from the foot surgery – getting in and out of shoes was agony – but he said he'd be

181

damned if he would shuffle out in slippers and conduct from a stool.)

The second week in February, he and the orchestra set off for Hong Kong – a twenty-five-hour trip each way. A reporter from KDKA, Pittsburgh's commercial television station, thrust a microphone in Previn's face just before he got on the plane, and asked, 'André, what about Hong Kong?'

Previn said, 'Hong Kong? My God. Well, it's farther than Aliquippa.' Aliquippa is a borough in western Pennsylvania.

The orchestra was warmly welcomed in Hong Kong and the concerts well-received, and there were the usual interviews. The *South China Morning Post* interviewed Previn and had this to say about him:

> André Previn, the Hollywood whiz kid, no longer exists. Nor, for that matter, does André Previn, the jet-setter with the boyish looks and penchant for gamine-faced actresses.
>
> In their place is a dedicated artist whose name is solidly identified with two of the world's greatest symphony orchestras – the Pittsburgh and the London.
>
> The charm and razor-sharp wit haven't vanished, though.
>
> As the undoubted star of this year's Arts Festival proved at a press conference yesterday, both are as potent as ever.
>
> What particular idiosyncrasy identified him as a conductor? asked one eager reporter. Was he like, say, von Karajan?
>
> 'No,' replied the maestro without missing a beat. 'I keep my eyes open.'
>
> At 54, André Previn has visibly mellowed. Gone is the trendy garb of the Mia Farrow era. In yesterday's 'working clothes' – sober black shirt and slacks and woolly jacket – he was conservatism itself. His personal life seems to be running along similar lines.

'My wife and I go absolutely everywhere together and I'm very sorry – for both selfish and altruistic reasons – that she couldn't come with me to Hong Kong. I know she would have loved it. Unfortunately it was impossible this time.'

There was the usual paragraph about the number of children Previn is financially responsible for – seven – and then this:

Now Lukas is enjoying centrestage, though so far there's been no hint of musical talent.
'We'll give him another shot at it in a few months, but nothing spectacular has happened yet,' smiles his father.

There was the usual paragraph about his career in Hollywood, and then this:

'People seem to find it harder to forgive me for writing film scores than they would if I was the Boston Strangler.'

There was an explanation of why he feels televised concerts are so important:

'Whether out of habit or geographic location, a lot of people don't go to concerts, but they are able to turn a knob.
'Using a medium like TV simply makes music accessible.'

And there was a final question about how it felt to be a celebrity:

'I've spent years wondering what makes certain conductors instantly and recognisably a box office draw,' admits the maestro.

The bitterly disappointed Previn fans who missed out on their idol when he caught measles and couldn't appear with the London Symphony at the 1974 Hongkong Arts Festival could probably explain.

So could those who have forked out $1,000 each for the privilege of attending tonight's 'Evening with André Previn' [a chamber-music concert] at the City Hall.

The *Hong Kong Standard* wrote:

The zest for life and *joie de vivre* expressed in the words and music of André Previn makes one feel he will remain a stranger to the domain of angst of aging.

CHAPTER 3

Previn's schedule seems designed to enable him to celebrate the birthdays of his children, and in February he came to New York to preside over a birthday party for the twins in Rumplemayer's. He stopped by my apartment on his way to the restaurant. Two of his children were with him – Lark and Soon-Yi. Pretty, well mannered little girls, they had obviously been told to be quiet, and they sat on a couch and played a card game noiselessly. Whichever one won received a swift kick from the loser. The scene was not lost on Previn, but it did not interfere with his talking about recent events.

Previn reported that having John Harbison in Pittsburgh had proved to be a godsend. 'He's terrific. He goes through scores sent to me, makes sense of things I can't, and pieces that I feel aren't right for me we send to David Atherton, in San Diego. He's great with modern music. John has a "Music Here and Now" series that's beginning to catch on, and he's almost finished a piece he's written for the Pittsburgh. I'll do it in May, for an American Festival we're planning. I also want to do his first symphony next year. Seiji commissioned it for the Boston, and I'm crazy about it.'

He lit a cigarette and said, 'The symphony got a new president in October, G. Christian Lantzsch. He suggested we have a series of meetings, and during those meetings I discovered he was a first-rate choice for president of a symphony society. He had done a lot of work, a lot of research. He had even gone to American Symphony Orchestra League meetings. And this was the realisation, evidently, of a long ambition of his. He said the magic words to me: "I think what we can do here in Pittsburgh is

make the orchestra this generation's Cleveland Orchestra."
I felt as if someone had handed me a rainbow.' He
glanced at his watch, and continued, 'I convinced the
board that we are in desperate need of a public-relations
person – someone with a tremendous amount of sophistication. Not for me, but for the orchestra. I did a lot of
research, and that which I already knew became obvious –
that Margaret Carson, in New York, is the best there is.
She came to Pittsburgh to hear several rehearsals and a
concert, and I had lunch with her. She told me, "There are
very few orchestras I've ever heard that are as good as
yours. The harsh thing is that nobody knows that. If you
played twice as good as the Berlin, the Boston, and the
Vienna combined, it still wouldn't do you any good,
unless people knew that. There's a big job to be done
here." I told Chris Lantzsch that she is the answer to a
prayer, and he agrees, so we are now putting that deal
together. I think she's funny and smart and wicked, and
she has an interesting mixture of love and cynicism about
music. The orchestra is ready to compete on the very
highest levels, but we have to convince the management
that there is more to it than just playing well. There's no
gainsaying the fact that a lot of money will have to be
spent to make the orchestra both national and international.
Our presence in New York should be taken for granted
every year, as is the case with the Chicago, the Cleveland,
the Boston. We should not come in and do normal
programmes. We should come in and do absolute *killers* –
the Britten *War Requiem*, a concert version of *Wozzeck*. And
that's all going to take a lot of just plain money.' (I had
heard that the Pittsburgh board hated to spend the money
for a work that required a big chorus when the orchestra
went to New York, and it turned out that it was at the
board's insistence that Previn have a big-name soloist. The
board feared the Pittsburgh and Previn couldn't fill either
hall in the city without that. But they underestimated their
conductor and the orchestra, too. William Lockwood, who
is in charge of the 'Great Performances' series at Avery

Fisher Hall, told me that Previn and the Pittsburgh, and certainly Previn, always sold out. His statement was proved when Ashkenazy was Previn's soloist one season. The concert was sold out well in advance. I asked Lockwood if that was because of Ashkenazy, and he said no. Sometimes Pittsburgh – which calls itself the City of Smiles – seemed like an extraordinarily beautiful woman with an inferiority complex – in constant need of re-assurance that she is indeed beautiful.)

I asked Previn if the board was aware of how he felt about Marshall, and he said, 'No, of course not. We *have* to be working colleagues. What's going to happen there I don't know. Chris realises that some fairly convulsive changes in attitude have to be made with management, and whether he can implement those with the current cast is not my business. It's up to him. In the meantime, I've been very flattered, because both the Los Angeles, which is losing Giulini, and the San Francisco, which is losing de Waart, have been after me to take their orchestras, and both Ernest Fleischmann, from LA – he hired me for the LSO all those years ago – and Peter Pastreich, from San Francisco, have come to Pittsburgh several times, and they've come backstage to see me in my dressing room, which management has to be aware of. Both of those orchestras are *very* good, but I have no desire to make the distance between England and the United States three thousand miles greater. More important, I *love* the Pitts-burgh Orchestra, and I've put in eight very hard years there. While management knows that two orchestras want me is a good time for me to get some things I want for the orchestra. I want more subsidisation of records, more television exposure, money for better guest conductors. I want a summer home for the orchestra. They shouldn't be playing all over the city, in wretched weather, in hellholes. There are a lot of things the board and management can do, for which they actually have the money, but they have to let *go* of it for a while. It's a very conservative board. They're sitting on an enormous trust fund, and they don't want to diminish it even temporarily. But they're going to have to.

'The people in the orchestra are aware that we can outplay most everybody – on a *good* night – and the only reason that it's so variable, with certain conductors, different situations, when it's not really that terrific, is because we haven't yet achieved that unspoken pride of place that a member of the Boston Symphony or the Vienna Philharmonic has, where they don't *allow* themselves to relax during a concert even if they *hate* the guest conductor or the music director or whatever. In order to achieve that, you have to make the orchestra feel more important. That's what we haven't got yet. While the board is very helpful – they really do work pretty hard for the orchestra – the city itself is not as civically involved in the welfare of the orchestra as I think they ought to be. I tried to tell the board the following far-fetched analogy: if in Chicago you stopped ten people on Michigan Boulevard and asked them to name some things that Chicago is well-known for I think seven out of ten would list the orchestra, and out of those seven I would be surprised if more than one has ever been to a concert. But they know that it is something of which Chicago is proud. That kind of involvement in the *non*-concertgoing public doesn't exist in Pittsburgh, and I think it can and it ought to. What gave me a kick – a couple of weeks ago, I got to the hall early, and I went to a good bakery that has coffee much better than the stuff that comes out of the machines in the hall, to get a coffee to go. The nice lady who waited on me said, "Are you going to the West Coast?" I said, "No", and she said, "I'm very glad." I told her that that was very nice of her, and asked if she went to very many of the concerts. She said she'd never been to a concert, and I said, "Well, forgive me – but what do *you* care?" She said, "I don't go to ball games, either, but I'm glad the Pirates and the Steelers are here." And I thought, "That's exactly what I'm talking about. That's what I want for the orchestra." She was a rare exception. That's very hard to achieve. I would like the orchestra to feel that no matter what other orchestra is having openings and auditions for those openings that they would not consider going to take those auditions, because they're already in as good a position as they can be. We don't have that yet. If Boston or Chicago or Cleveland has an opening for a good position, very often our players will go and take the audition. And I don't like that. I don't like the idea that we're an interim step for musicians. I think it should be an ultimate step. That kind of joy in playing in a specific orchestra can only be achieved if the orchestra is quite obviously an international treasure. As Margaret Carson said, musically we may be, but nobody knows that. So until the musicians can feel that everybody in that city is aware of the orchestra they're always going to go and take auditions, and I'm going to lose valuable players. I have two *first-rate* players who are going to audition for the Cleveland, and there's nothing I can do to stop them, and that's a shame.'

I said, 'You can hope they don't make it', and he said, 'Well, you see, that's where I'm torn.'

CHAPTER 4

On 18 March, Previn went to Berlin to conduct two concerts with the Berlin Philharmonic. Although he had told the students at Tanglewood that Rachmaninoff was not appreciated in Germany, his soloist, Vladimir Ashkenazy, played that composer's Fourth Concerto. Previn said, by way of explanation, 'They're so crazy about Ashkenazy that he can play anything he wants to. They just want to hear him.' The critics, as it turned out, were crazy about Previn.

Walter Kaempfer wrote, in *Der Tagespiegel*,

It doesn't happen often that one meets a conductor of such sovereign perfection, such technically perfect directions to the orchestra, and a virtuosity of stick technique which is at the same time minutely precise and flowingly emotional. Every nuance of colour and dynamics merits his attention.

A review signed 'W. Sch.', in the *Berliner Morgenpost*, said,

These were extraordinary performances, performances of the absolute first rank. One will hold them in memory for a long time.

The manner in which André Previn conducted the most sensuous score Ravel ever wrote (Daphnis and Chloe) was worthy of being a model. He does away with all surface effects, or washes of impressionistic sound. He insists on precision, transparency and strength. He leads the orchestra in his own seemingly nonchalant way, but achieves orchestral sounds which are wonderfully lithe, sometimes overwhelming and

190

rhythmically animated in every blink of the eye. His interpretations of Ravel and Rachmaninov swept the listeners away and one will not hear the like of them again soon.

Also in Berlin with Previn was a television crew from CBS, which had come there to film a segment on Previn for the Bill Moyers-Charles Kuralt television programme 'Crossroads'. The crew also went to Surrey: the producer, David Burke; the associate producer, Elizabeth Karnes; the correspondent, Andrew Lack; and the cameraman, Jon Peters. (Miss Karnes and Peters had already been to Pittsburgh, and they returned with a lot of film of Previn conducting the Pittsburgh Symphony Orchestra.) In Surrey, Burke got more footage than he would probably need: Previn strolling through the grounds with Heather and Lack; tootling around the vast lawn on a red lawn mower that looked like a small tractor, with Heather, who had shown him how to turn it on, as a passenger; talking to Lack in the living-room of the two-hundred-and-fifty-year-old house (the thatched-roof guest-cottage was not in view); playing the piano for five-month-old Lukas, a healthy, jolly baby with uncommon presence, who grabbed his famous father by the nose and held tight. It was easy to see why Previn loved the place so much. It was a quiet explosion of beauty – banks of multicoloured blossoming bushes bordering the sweeping lawn, with meadow and forest beyond. (When Previn bought the place, a representative of the local gentry came to see him and told him that they were accustomed to riding to hounds on Previn's twenty acres; they assumed he wouldn't mind if they continued to do so. Previn said, 'Not at all. Not as long as they don't mind being shot at.')

On 23 March, Previn got a call from Peter Pastreich, the managing director of the San Francisco Symphony, telling him that Marshall Turkin had been fired. Previn was thunderstruck. He asked how Pastreich knew, and Pastreich said, 'Marshall told me himself. He just called. He's calling everyone.' Pastreich had called to say that he assumed that Previn would be staying in Pittsburgh, and that the San Francisco, which had had a gentleman's agreement with Herbert Blomstedt, had hired him.

Lantzsch had periodically been reporting to Previn about the Turkin situation. According to an account in *Pittsburgh Magazine*, written by John Spitzer, summing up what happened:

> Between December and the following March, Lantzsch scrutinized Turkin's activities and asked him to present reports about management operations. At the end of the evaluation, on Friday, March 23, Lantzsch called Turkin into his office and informed him that his contract, which was to run out in October, 1984, would not be renewed. Only hours before, at a hastily scheduled meeting of the Executive Committee of the Symphony's Board of Directors, Lantzsch had secured approval to let Turkin's contract lapse.

Now Lantzsch, too, called Previn and told him, 'I've just had the most amazing afternoon. I just fired Marshall.' Previn said, 'Just like that?' and Lantzsch said, 'Just like that.'

On the 27th, Lantzsch called again. He said he had some peculiar news: the Executive Committee changed its mind, and rehired Marshall. In fact, they had given him a new four-year contract. Previn repeated the conversation to me. He said to Lantzsch, ' "Didn't you *fire* him at the request of the Executive Committee?" Chris said yes, but over the weekend they changed their minds. I asked, "What's going to happen now? By now, he knows that I dislike him, the orchestra dislikes him, and *you* dislike him." Chris said, "Marshall is not to have anything to do with the music director, the orchestra, their comings and goings, deals, contracts, and, this being the year of the musicians' new contract, he's not to have anything to do with that. He'll do market research, long-range planning

192

for a summer home." I suggested that it might be simpler to pay him off, what they call the "golden handshake". But they didn't want to do that. [People close to what was happening said that Turkin's contract had a 'golden parachute' clause – fifty thousand dollars a year for ten years when he left – and the handshake would have been a five-hundred-thousand-dollar one.] I asked who they thought would manage all the things Marshall was *not* going to manage. Chris said they'd get somebody. I said, "With all deference, you're going to have a hell of a time with that, because Marshall's going to keep his title; he will be working with the board. Where are you going to find a first-rate man who is going to come in (a) having to wait four years before assuming the title of the job which he has already been holding down, and (b) during those four years being answerable to Marshall. You have to face it. Marshall has a terrible reputation right now." Chris said they'd find someone somehow, and for the orchestra's psychological wellbeing Marshall would be moved out of his office, be removed from the floor where the orchestra's artistic wellbeing is seen to. It didn't seem workable to me.' What Spitzer revealed in his article, and Lantzsch did not tell Previn, was that several of the Executive Committee members – including Robert Buckley – had missed that Friday meeting, and over the weekend they were 'galvanised into action' to save Turkin.

Next, Ernest Fleischmann called. He said to Previn, 'Now that I hear Marshall's been fired, I guess that means LA is up a creek.'

Previn said, 'If you'd called me ten minutes ago, I would have said yes. But, no.' Previn told Fleischmann what had happened, and Fleischmann said, 'I'm coming to see you. Someone has to begin to talk some sense to you.'

Previn went to Vienna on the first of April for two weeks of conducting and recording with the Vienna Philharmonic. (He is one of only eight conductors whom that venerable institution will work with.) Both Ronald Wilford and Fleischmann came to Vienna to discuss

Previn's future. Wilford felt Previn would not be happy in Los Angeles – that the press would have him for breakfast, lunch, and dinner, rehashing his past, dredging up movies and marriages and romances. Fleischmann felt that the Pittsburgh situation was impossible. Both men were aware of the fact that Previn was tenacious in his desire to hang on to the Pittsburgh. Wilford said he would go to Pittsburgh again to see if he could arrive at a workable situation for Previn. Fleischmann presented a very strong case for Previn's going to Los Angeles. He began talking terms with him, and the offer was so attractive that it outweighed the negative aspects that Wilford had brought up. Although Fleischmann flew home with high hopes, there was a quiet, nagging fear that Pittsburgh might still, somehow, win the deeply hurt Previn back.

CBS came to Vienna and filmed Previn conducting the Philharmonic and recording two Mozart concertos with the orchestra, and then packed up and went home, and, as often happens with a television crew, they missed a nice scene. Heather arrived in Vienna for the second week of Previn's conducting there, and with her were Lukas and Lukas's nanny. (Heather says she buys all her clothes in Vienna, because they are so beautifully made, and she has an elegant, understated look: she wears the clothes, they don't wear her.) One day, they all went shopping, and Heather saw a little suit in a shop window that she wanted to buy for the baby. They went into the shop, and Heather started to tell the salesgirl what she wanted, but there was a language barrier: the girl didn't speak English or French. Previn had been waiting near the door, and he stepped up to the counter and, in rapid-fire German, proceeded to tell the girl what Heather wanted, and to complete the purchase. The shop was small and rather stuffy, and Heather told Previn that she and the nanny would wait for him outside, with the baby. Five minutes later, Previn, laughing maniacally, came out. The salesgirl had asked him if he did 'this kind of thing often'. Previn

194

asked, 'What kind of thing?' She said, 'Guide tourists around, bring them into shops, translate for them.' Previn said, 'Occasionally', at which the girl slyly slipped him a folded-up fifty-schilling note. Previn thanked her, tucked the bill in his pocket, and left.

Back in England, Previn practised and recorded day and night with the Musikverein Quartet, composed of the principals from the Vienna Philharmonic, and then he had free time – time to worry. Heather reported that he was in a terrible state. She said, 'The board is divided and divisive. He fears that he'll have to fight for everything he wants, and there will always be the one or two decisive, ambivalent votes. There's talk of getting a go-between, an assistant manager, or whatever, but who worth his salt would take such a job? André's feelings have been badly hurt. I feel so sorry for him. He's snappy, nervous. He can't sleep. Poor bloke.' Heather had blown the contents out of twenty-two eggs for a family Easter-egg-painting contest, and Previn had stopped pacing the floor and brooding long enough to paint an egg that was colourful enough to disguise his feeling that he was about to lose something, family excepted, that was most precious to him.

CHAPTER 5

It was all over New York, according to Margaret Carson, that Previn was going to Los Angeles. The week before Previn's return to Pittsburgh, Marshall Turkin had come to New York, hat in hand, to see Mrs Carson. She was touched by his humility and honesty. He told her that he had been fired and rehired, and he hoped she would do publicity for the Pittsburgh. Mrs Carson was noncommittal. She was beginning to feel she was more interested in promoting Previn than the Pittsburgh – that the latter would be extremely difficult to promote without Previn. Mrs Carson had a number of things to consider. Along with the rumours that Previn was leaving Pittsburgh were rumours about who would take his place, and one of the names mentioned frequently was that of Michael Tilson Thomas, a client of Mrs Carson's. The Los Angeles had been a client until Giulini resigned. She turned to Ronald Wilford. Unlike the Cabots and the Lodges, Ronald Wilford, who is married to a Whitney, speaks to no one, according to his assistant, Judi Janowsky, and this attitude annoys a great many people – even people who don't especially want to speak to him. Mrs Carson is an exception to his sweeping rule, because she is in what she calls 'the trade'. Wilford told her that he was going to Pittsburgh one more time, and he hoped to work things out in a way that no one would get hurt. (Previn is so fond of Wilford that he asked him to be Lukas's godfather.)

On Tuesday morning, Previn met with Wilford, Lantzsch, and Robert Buckley in his quarters at Heinz Hall. Previn left the meeting to rehearse the orchestra, and, according to John Spitzer, 'The meeting was inconclusive.'

Previn told me that Lantzsch called him at home that night and asked him not to do anything hasty. Lantzsch hoped to have one more meeting with the Executive Committee on Friday to work something out that would keep Previn in Pittsburgh. (Turkin was still in his office on the fifth floor, and it was business as usual.) Previn said, 'I then gambled my job. I said, "If you can work it out, fine." And the other thing I made very sure that Chris understood was that if Marshall's problems with me were the only problems that he had, then he wouldn't *have* a problem. I can get along with anybody. I dislike him personally, but that's got nothing to do with anything. The week went by in utter silence, the Executive Committee meeting was never called, and Saturday morning Chris called and said, "I understand you're going to talk to the orchestra tonight and tender your resignation." I *told* them I would do that unless I heard from them with some kind of new plan. I waited all week long, like someone on Death Row.' He told Cecie Sommers, vice-president and Programme Director of WQED-FM, that he felt as if he were living in the middle of a Kafka novel.

That night, before the concert, Previn was in his dressing room when Marshall Turkin appeared. It was the first time Previn had seen him since his return to Pittsburgh. Turkin gave Previn a firm handshake and said, 'Good luck tonight.' After he left, Sid Kaplan came in.

Previn said, 'Kappy, make damn sure that man is not around when I talk to the orchestra after the concert.'

Kappy said, 'Don't worry. He just went home.'

After the concert, Previn met with the orchestra members in the big practice room on the fourth floor. He told them 'I'd written a speech, but you know me well enough to know I don't really give speeches.' Actually, he spoke to them as he would a room full of friends. He told them that when the board fired and then rehired Turkin, it indicated to him a divided board – something no music director could work with profitably or comfortably. He told them that he had decided to go to Los Angeles, and he was sorry that they'd been put through this period of doubt and rumours and conflict, especially at this time, with negotiations for new contracts coming up. He said, 'You understand that this has nothing to do with just Marshall and me, because that's silly.' Several women had begun to weep, and he concluded, 'With all my heart, I had hoped to stay in Pittsburgh. Now I'm going to ask that there be no questions, because my *guts* just can't take it.' When Previn began his talk, an orchestra member slipped out and called the press, and it was a source of annoyance to the Executive Committee that the news that Previn was leaving Pittsburgh broke in New York, Los Angeles, and Pittsburgh simultaneously.

Preceding Previn's resignation by three days was the announcement in both Pittsburgh papers that John Harbison had been dismissed as composer-in-residence. His funded two-year term was up, and John Duffy – who has said that the Pittsburgh programme had been so successful that it was second only to the New York Philharmonic's Horizons '84 – proposed a third year, with 'Meet the Composer' providing half of Harbison's salary and the Pittsburgh Symphony the other half – twenty thousand dollars from each organisation. Previn had written to MIT, where Harbison is a chaired professor, asking to have Harbison for another year, and early in 1984 Turkin had written Harbison a letter saying that his third year in Pittsburgh was 'all set', 'subject to the committee's approval of his schedule'. But the week Harbison was dumped Turkin phoned him 'to tell him his appointment was not approved, the chief reason offered being that he did not conform to availability guidelines'. (Robert Croan and Marylynn Uricchio, of the *Post-Gazette*, wrote the chronicle being quoted.) A stunned Harbison said, 'I had asked to be in Pittsburgh seven and a half instead of eight months. . . No one ever called me to say I should change my schedule. If they had, I would have changed it. It was only a difference of two weeks.' Turkin told Lantzsch that 'Meet the Composer' had to be cancelled because of Previn's planned six-month sabbatical in 1984. John Duffy told me that that point was never raised or discussed and had nothing to do with anything. Duffy is one of those people in the general field of music promotion who love music so much that there is not anything they would not do to further its cause. Turkin told Duffy that the board had approved Harbison's third year but that Previn had nixed it.

Harbison and Previn had become good friends, and Harbison and his wife, Rosemary, both suffered a great deal before they arrived at a clear understanding of what had happened – realised that Previn had not betrayed them. Turkin's final statement to the press on the subject of Harbison was that the composer would continue on in Pittsburgh as a consultant. But he failed to talk this over with Harbison, and the subjects of time and money were never gone into. Harbison had relatives in Pittsburgh who had helped sustain him and his wife through this difficult emotional period, and they left town with the feeling that, if it weren't for their relatives, they would just as soon not even fly *over* that city, much less drop in so Harbison could participate in programming. Harbison, a tall, handsome, distinguished-looking man ('professorial,' Heather Previn says; 'I can see him, in academic robes, flapping across the quadrangle at Cambridge') commented, 'Someday some-one will do a Ph.D thesis on what happened in Pittsburgh. It will be 'How Not to Run an Orchestra'. (Rosemary Harbison is a violinist who has put her own career on hold, for the time being, and is strongly supportive of her husband. She could tell that Ph.D thesis-writer a great deal about what happened in Pittsburgh, but, for the moment, she only wanted to speak about Previn: 'I came away from this experience with an uncommon respect and affection for this man. I don't know, in my experience, of any other situation in which a composer who is a colleague has the kind of generosity and real vision – a

199

capacity for that vision of music that André Previn has. One is speechless with a man of this talent and generosity; truly one of the most unique people walking the planet.')

The forty-odd symphony board members who were not on the Executive Committee found themselves in the odd position of reading about what was happening in the newspapers, instead of knowing about it first-hand. There were countless rumours – one of them that Harbison was a trade-off for Margaret Carson. Both local papers were flooded with letters to the editor, editorials, and lengthy accounts – mostly guesswork – of what was going on, and mostly pro-Previn.

Previn was angry about what happened to Harbison. He said, 'It's an admission of provincialism not to keep him. The "Composer in Residence" programme is the first time since Koussevitzky that composers have been treated as part of an orchestra's wellbeing. This will get back to the National Endowment for the Arts, which a couple of years ago said, "You guys have got so much money anyway that we'd rather spend it on more needy orchestras." Pittsburgh has a forty-five-million-dollar endowment fund, which is the highest in the country. The NEA will take whatever is left away from the Pittsburgh, and our reputation will be somewhat like Dayton, Ohio. It's unbelievable that they don't see that – *refuse* to see it. Don't *want* to see it. It's mind-bogglingly stupid.'

For Previn, the timing of the 'Saturday-night massacre', as some orchestra members came to call the night of his resignation, could not have happened at a worse time. The following day, there would be a seven-hour fund-raising telethon, and in addition to the afternoon concert – which would include the Shostakovich Concerto No. 1 for Cello and Orchestra, with Yo-Yo Ma as soloist, and the Mussorgsky/Ravel 'Pictures at an Exhibition' – there would be the final evening chamber-music concert, and Previn would perform the three programmed works with members of the orchestra and Mr Ma. (The series had been successful beyond Previn's wildest dreams. He had been moved by the excellence of the nearly anonymous musicians who had come to the fore and performed, and someone from the Minnesota Orchestra who heard one of the concerts told him, 'Very few orchestras have such excellent players – players who can shine in solo roles.') Yo-Yo Ma loved the orchestra, and all week he had been begging Previn not to leave.

Also, coming up, beginning the weekend of 11 May, was the American Festival – three weeks of American music in Heinz Hall, followed by a tour of three cities, New York, Washington, and Toronto. Previn would be conducting the premieres of five works, including John Harbison's 'Ulysses' Bow', written for the Pittsburgh, and conducting and playing Gershwin's 'Rhapsody in Blue' and his Concerto in F, and at the end of the tour Previn would record the Harbison piece. So in addition to preparing the Shostakovich and Mussorgsky he'd been busy studying the five premiere pieces. Even he gasped at the workload.

Some people thought the telethon was less than successful. The phones didn't ring all that often, which could have been attributed to the fact that it was a beautiful, sunny day in Pittsburgh – the first after weeks of cold, gloomy rain. Cecie Sommers, who runs fund-raisers for WQED, said, 'They don't know how to run a telethon down there. When we do one, we get five hundred dollars for a cheesecake. They can't understand why anyone would pay five hundred dollars for a cheesecake.' Mrs Sommers may have been biased. Marshall Turkin had soured relations between the orchestra and the public-broadcasting station. There had been three additional 'Previn and the Pittsburgh' broadcasts – Previn's jazz session with Perlman, Manne, Mitchell, and Hall; the British Festival; and Horacio Gutiérrez, playing the Rach-maninoff third piano concerto. Turkin took the proposal for the programmes, written and printed at WQED, to

London, where he tried to engage Ian Englemann to come to Pittsburgh to produce and direct the programmes, using the facilities of KDKA. When Englemann found out that WQED would be excluded from the project, he smelled foul politics. Back in Pittsburgh, a spokesperson for Gulf Oil, one of the sponsors, explained to Turkin that WQED was included in the funding – that without WQED there would be no money and no programmes. Lloyd Kaiser, WQED's president, who loves the city and the orchestra and would do anything to promote fragile culture there, and who is accustomed to dealing with people of principles, laughed explosively when I asked him if Turkin's behaviour was ethical. Kaiser said, 'Let's say it was highly unusual.' (Turkin's behaviour at times was folkloric. At receptions in Europe he called American ambassadors 'Mr President.' And as often as Previn cautioned him – *coached* him – he could not remember to address a lord correctly. He called them Mister, too, and then garbled the last name. Possibly there were times when the ease with which Previn moved from one world to another irked him. After a concert in Montreal, at a reception, the Canadian cultural attaché addressed the gathering in English and then in French, and Previn responded in kind. In Pittsburgh, Count Basie leapt out of a cab when he saw Previn and said, 'Hi, big daddy!' Previn said, 'Hey, my man!' and the two exchanged the familiar hand-slap.)

One prize the telethon people hoped to offer was a weekend in New York that would include a personal guided tour of the Metropolitan Opera House, the personal guide being Dinah Daniels, who had gone to work for the Met after Turkin fired her. Miss Daniels and Stephen Dick, the producer of the original, bumper crop of 'Previn and the Pittsburgh' broadcasts, married in 1982 and were living in New York. (Of the Executive Committee's action in firing and rehiring Turkin, Dick said, 'André will be better off in Los Angeles. But what a slap in the face.') The telethon request had evoked peals of Swiss-bell laughter from Miss Daniels. She declined.

Previn said that the only thing that got him through this period was the fact that Heather and the baby were with him. Lantzsch met with the orchestra – he asked that Previn not be there – and told them a search committee for a new music director had been formed, and Marshall Turkin would be the advisor. A scheduled 'Previn and the Pittsburgh' broadcast of the American Festival was cancelled. (The sponsor was Allegheny International.) Turkin, without Previn's knowledge, flew to Vienna and tried to engage Lorin Maazel as a replacement for Previn. Maazel had left the Cleveland to be the music director of the Vienna State Opera, but, like Karajan and others, he was so brutalised by that company's management that he quit after little more than a year. The Pittsburgh would have been a step down for him, but he agreed to act as a consultant. Previn said that every day something nasty happened, and on 8 May he asked to be released from the remaining two years of his contract.

CHAPTER 6

On May 19th's Saturday-night concert, Previn conducted the premiere of John Harbison's 'Ulysses' Bow'. Previn said of the piece, 'I hope in future my c.v. will include the fact that I conducted the first performance of that piece.' The concert was Previn's last Saturday series event in Pittsburgh, and Heather Previn thought someone should mark the occasion, so at concert's end she presented her husband with a bouquet of roses on stage. He got a standing ovation, as he had after every concert since the news of his resignation.

Previn said, 'I was so tired that night I wondered if I could even make it home, and Heather reminded me that we'd promised to have a drink with Annie and Randy and Harold. Not far away. She said they'd meet us in one of the rooms in the hall. I put on my usual jeans and sneakers, and we went into the room, and Holy Christ! There were hundreds of people – orchestra members and wives and girlfriends, dressed to the teeth, yelling and clapping. They had rented the hall, paid for a huge dinner, tablecloths, flowers, wine, booze. One of the principals, Howard Hillyer, the first horn, gave a truly funny speech, and gave me all kinds of insane presents: an LA Dodgers hat, and a mask for smog, and a hopelessly beaten up French horn, and a baton covered with rhinestones. And then Al Hirtz, a violinist, got up and said, "It's not easy to think of a present for you, but we decided on the *Oxford English Dictionary*." I've never in my life seen it in private ownership – only in libraries. It is quite without a double the best set of reference books ever devised. In my *lifetime* such an expensive gesture from an orchestra is absolutely unheard of.' The orchestra gave

204

Previn a small dictionary, representing the OED, with a plaque. The sixteen volumes would be shipped to Surrey.

Sunday, Heather got to the hall early – well before the afternoon concert would begin. She brought long-stemmed roses, and put one for each musician, and a card with the musicians's name, on the stands. Then she went up to the balcony and looked down on the empty stage. She said, 'I've never seen anything so sad in my life.' Beverly Morrow, who is in charge of media relations for the Pittsburgh, alerted the press to the fact that Previn had been getting standing ovations and that this would be his last concert with the orchestra in Heinz Hall, and there were a number of photographers in the hall. The programme included the premiere of Raymond Premru's 'Celebrations'; William Schuman's Symphony No. 3; Aaron Copland's 'Connotations'; and George Gershwin's 'Rhapsody in Blue'. At the conclusion, the applause was thunderous, and the orchestra refused to stand when Previn gave them the familiar gesture. Finally, after repeated curtain calls, he raised his hands to the audience, asking for silence. When the audience was quiet, Previn said, 'It does not matter who is conductor. What matters is the orchestra. If you would do me a great favour, I will leave the stage and you can applaud your sensational Pittsburgh orchestra.' He left the stage and the audience stood and applauded the orchestra. The ovation was so prolonged that finally Previn went out one more time, and then he led the orchestra off.

On Monday, Heather flew to Surrey with Lukas. His paediatrician said he should not be flying to New York, Washington, Toronto, and back to Pittsburgh; all those takeoffs and landings would be hard on the baby's ears. I saw her in TWA's Ambassadors' Lounge, at Kennedy Airport, where she had three hours to kill before the flight to London. From her own childhood experiences of travelling all over the world, Heather tries to make Lukas at home and happy wherever he is. Propped in the corner of a soft armchair, with a favourite stuffed toy next to him, he seemed to survey the room with poise. He was more calm than cranky, and when his mother left him to go to the desk to make seat reservations he didn't howl but, rather, gurgled complacently. He was a big, blond, blue-eyed infant who would soon earn the nickname Chubbs. He was, as Previn had said, a knockout.

Heather looked sad. She said, 'André loved that orchestra so much – and to have the whole thing just blow up. . . It was a miscalculation, basically. Chris Lantzsch thought he could work out the deal that he and André wanted – to make the orchestra terrific. Two or three board members have an absolute stranglehold on the others. They're the ones who are responsible for the screw-up. They don't want the orchestra to go forward. It costs too much, in terms of money and effort. They want to run the orchestra like a business – which, in a way, is how all orchestras are run. They're all sponsored by big business. They don't have any feeling for the end product. It's not a sheet of aluminium. It's people with hearts and souls.' She paused for a second, and then said, 'The way you and I feel about Rostropovich, Giulini, Heifetz – Marshall feels about people with great wealth. He's absolutely in awe of them. But it's too easy to say that he's the villain. He's a victim, the same as André. Look at him. He's without a music director. They're going to find out that without someone like André, someone who loves the orchestra, they're going to fall apart.'

Heather fed Lukas baby-food peach cobbler as she talked. She said, 'André did them a favour in leaving. Now it will be clear to everyone how that board works. His leaving, the manner in which he's leaving, has revealed the strange way in which the board operates. The board is reticent about telling the truth about what happened; they'll look like fools when the truth comes out. André will be happy to be out of that small-town way of thinking, but musically he'll be very sad for a very long

206

time. They were just at the point of true excellence. The concerts this month have been out of this world.'

She changed the subject. 'We're having an addition built – a new dining-room in Surrey. André wants the kind he remembers from his childhood. Heavy furniture, heavy glasses, white linen tablecloths, napkins. It's the first time he's talked much about his childhood. To make up for the heavy furniture, I get lots of windows. I'm going to bring the beauty of the garden inside – pale creams and lovely greens.' Her flight was announced, and she gathered Lukas and all the paraphernalia together and I walked with her to the gate. She was thinking about Pittsburgh again, and her parting words were 'I blame two or three of those board members with a *vengeance*.'

On Tuesday, 22 May, Previn took the Pittsburgh on the American Tour. The first stop was the Kennedy Center, in Washington, DC. Ernest Fleischmann flew to Washington, bringing with him two members of the Los Angeles Philharmonic Orchestra board of directors. After the concert, Previn had dinner with Fleischmann and the board members. In New York, the orchestra played in Avery Fisher Hall and Carnegie Hall. In Avery Fisher, Previn conducted 'Ulysses' Bow' and played and conducted from the keyboard the Gershwin Concerto in F. In a first-tier box, to the left of the stage, Matthew, Sascha, Fletcher, Soon-Yi, Lark, and Daisy Previn happily and enthusiastically applauded their father after the concerto. Previn waved and smiled at them. In the greenroom, Previn and Harbison accepted congratulations from a dense crowd of fans and friends. Threading his way through the throng, shaking every hand he could grab, was Marshall Turkin. He drew Harbison aside and said, 'I know you're worried about your symphony's not being performed next season. I'll get Michael Tilson Thomas to conduct it. He'd do *anything* to get the Pittsburgh.'

In Carnegie Hall, Previn conducted Aaron Copland's

'Connotations'; Richard Stoltzman played that composer's clarinet concerto; and Previn played 'Rhapsody in Blue'. He said of the performance of 'Connotations', 'It's *fearsomely* difficult to play. Those rehearsals were really quite something. But the orchestra wound up playing it fabulously well. Copland was there, and he said to me that it was the first time he'd heard all the notes and rhythms right. It was a great occasion. The hall was sold out, I got him to take a bow, and I have very rarely heard an audience go so wild about a composer. He's more than due that kind of thing, and it was wonderful to be part of it.'

After the concert, in the greenroom, Previn saw Turkin for the last time. Turkin shook his hand and said, 'I still think you're very talented.'

The final tour stop was Toronto, where the Pittsburgh gave two concerts in Roy Thompson Hall. They all returned to Pittsburgh Sunday morning, and for the rest of Sunday and all day Monday Previn began to empty his mountainside apartment. Everything was separated into two categories: things to be moved to Los Angeles and put into storage there, and things to be shipped to Surrey. He dreaded Tuesday. He would record the Harbison, and it would be the last time he would conduct the Pittsburgh.

Tuesday morning, Previn, Harbison, the orchestra, and a producer and an engineer from Nonesuch Records, the company that had contracted to record 'Ulysses' Bow', gathered in Heinz Hall. The piece is thirty-two minutes long, and both the composer and Previn thought it would be a tight squeeze completing the recording in the allotted four hours. Now the Nonesuch producer told them it would have to be done in three hours.

Previn told me, 'I asked him on whose orders, and he said, "Management." *Smoke* was coming out of my ears. I tried to get a name out of him – *who* in management, but he couldn't say.'

After the session was over, a number of musicians came in to say goodbye. One man, known for his reserve, said,

'I know that men in this country aren't supposed to hug, but to hell with that', and gave Previn a big hug. Another came in to say goodbye, and ended up in tears.

Wednesday morning, in the Hilton Hotel, where Previn spent his last night in the city, the critic Carl Apone interviewed him in an attempt to write a final summing-up of what had happened. (The account appeared in the *Pittsburgh Press* Sunday supplement, and a reproduction of Previn's signature headed each page. For the first time in eight years the acute accent appeared in 'André'.) Apone later wrote that although Previn said he didn't want to talk about it, he kept veering back to the subject of what had happened. Apone concluded that if Previn was faking his deep sadness at losing his orchestra, his four Academy Awards should have been for acting, not composing.

CHAPTER 7

When Previn resigned from the Pittsburgh, his move was commented on by a number of publications outside Pittsburgh. Thor Eckert, Jr, wrote, in the *Christian Science Monitor*, that

> André Previn may not be irreplaceable, but the exceptional results he has achieved with the Pittsburgh speak for themselves. And his recordings have put the orchestra back on the map as a viable musical force in this land. But to the board there – as so often with arts boards on this continent – internal social standings and power-playing are more important than the well-being of the institution it is supposedly dedicated to nurturing and sustaining. So now the board has allowed Previn to walk away because the pro-manager faction was stronger than the pro-music-director one.

Michael Walsh wrote, in *Time* magazine, 'Previn's departure from Pittsburgh was sealed when he lost an ugly power struggle with Managing Director Marshall Turkin over the orchestra's artistic direction, a rupture that Previn declines to confirm. "To lose a job is one thing, but to keep your manners has to be done at the same time." '

Some people say that Turkin's triumph represented the first time in history that a managing director won out over a music director, and there was a lot of understandable curiosity in music circles about Turkin. Who was he? Turkin tended to say 'no comment' to reporters or else claim that his relationship with Previn was productive, the record spoke for itself. John Spitzer got Turkin to talk by telling him he was interested in writing about him, not Previn, and Turkin talked; he had begun his career in

210

music as a composer, and he studied at Juilliard (though Juilliard had no record of Turkin's attending classes there). The late John Edwards, the dean of all managing directors in America until his death in August of 1984, said that Turkin had composed enough to qualify him for membership in ASCAP. Turkin came to Pittsburgh from Detroit, recommended to the board by Seymour Rosen after the board fired Rosen. Spitzer described Turkin:

> Dressed casually for a Saturday morning interview, Turkin looks wonderfully fit for his 58 years. His deep tan and chiseled musculature suggest an obsession with physical culture acquired during his days as manager of the Honolulu Symphony. But in his rapid speech and animated manner, there is a broad hint of Saul Bellow's Chicago, where he was born. . .

Spitzer commented on Turkin the composer:

> 'I was not a frustrated composer,' Turkin insists. Rather, the satisfaction he got from composing was 'transferred' to his career as a manager. Turkin tells the story of the first time he worked out a 'spread sheet' in cost accounting.
> 'It was like a score,' says Turkin with a note of wonder in his voice. 'I found it a creative process. . . the excitement as you worked out horizontally and then vertically. . . It was like counterpoint.'

At one point, Spitzer summarised the situation:

> The story of Turkin's dismissal and reinstatement, as well as the rumors of the Turkin-Previn fight, circulated rapidly and widely in the small world of American orchestras and orchestra management, and have done extensive damage to the reputation of the Pittsburgh Symphony. The story makes it seem as though Turkin was responsible for driving André Previn out of

211

Pittsburgh. It paints a picture of an administration unsympathetic to artistic goals, of a Board of Directors in disarray and a Symphony management too weak to carry out consistent policies.

And there was much, much more. Spitzer's article concluded:

> The manager not only has to cooperate with the Music Director and with the Board; in many cases he has to lead them both. Marshall Turkin's response to a question about leadership is striking:
> Pgh. Mag: How much of a leader is an orchestra manager?
> Turkin: Leader? What do you mean?
> Pgh. Mag: In the direction the orchestra takes, in relations with the conductor and with the Board. Do you see yourself as an independent agent?
> Turkin: Independent agent? No way! No. No. I'm hired and fired by a Board which represents the citizens, represents the community. And I report to them. I'm not an independent agent at all.
> The controversy and the rumors surrounding Previn's departure may have made it impossible for Turkin to do much leading in any case. He puts the best face on matters and marches resolutely, if a bit stiffly, ahead, towards a new conductor somewhere in the future, insisting all the while that everything is under control, that the Pittsburgh Symphony is a "world-class" orchestra.

I spoke to John Edwards, the managing director of the Chicago Symphony Orchestra, a week or so before his untimely, unexpected death. (He left no relatives, but a host of friends and colleagues all over the world who could not adequately express how valuable he was in the music field, how much he was loved, and how much he would be missed.) Edwards said of his role as a managing

212

director, 'I'm a father-confessor, marriage counsellor, psychiatrist, soft shoulder, financial advisor, anything musicians want that will make them happy.' Edwards was an assistant manager for two periods in Pittsburgh, and thought 'provincial' was the adjective that best describes that city. He knew Turkin well, and had this to say about him: 'I can't believe that Marshall was truly as gauche as he acted. I can't believe he was that stupid. I think it was part of a publican attitude. I think he was trying to shock people.'

I spoke to Previn the Sunday night he was in his apartment, sorting out his possessions, preparing to leave. He said, 'That last Sunday-afternoon concert, when I gestured to the audience for silence, several principals had a clear view of Marshall, sitting in a box with a couple of bigwigs. They told me that when I signalled for silence, Marshall appeared about to fling himself from the box. He clearly thought I was going to make a big speech, and tell the audience everything. How could anyone possibly *misread* me so?'

The press accounts of what happened revealed a great deal of ambivalence, and columnists seemed to write *around* what had happened. Previn's explanation of this was to say, 'There's a daisy chain of fear there. People are afraid they'll lose their jobs.' But the fear went beyond that. Some were busy guarding their image in the city – their importance. Some people said that if Lantzsch had been No. 1 at Mellon Bank, instead of just No. 2, the decision would have gone his way. As it was, he did an about-face, and lost twelve pounds in the process. Previn said of Lantzsch, 'He had some wonderful ideas, but the ball was taken away from him.' Even Joan Apt, who was on the board but not the Executive Committee, while deploring what had happened, refused to be quoted, in deference to other cultural projects she supported.

Orchestra members were questioned about how they felt, and most were full of praise for Previn. But, with contract negotiations coming up, they wanted to deal from

213

a position of united strength, and the ones I talked to tried to be philosophical. Musicians are, after all, like foster children, with their own bank accounts, at the mercy of an erratic welfare department. They could only hope for a new conductor they could respect and even like. One who would stick around for a few years – if they liked him. A lot of people chose to believe that Previn never wanted to stay in the city – that he'd always intended to use Pittsburgh as a stepping stone – people who would switch from one firm to another without hesitation, if the second offered a better position. Previn said, 'They're going to try to make me the villain in this, but it will be very hard for them to do that.' One young man had the courage to speak out – Barry Paris, a reporter for the *Post-Gazette*. His commentary was broadcast over WQED-FM – a multiple broadcast, repeated a number of times over the weekend. Paris said, in part.

If you haven't read the Previn-Pittsburgh Symphony article in the new issue of *Pittsburgh* magazine, you really should, not because of any bombshell revelation but because it's the clearest chronology of the confusing set of circumstances that resulted in the maestro's departure. So much has already been said and written on the subject, and yet so little of it has told the truth. The *Pittsburgh* article forces us to give it one last, sad reflection.

Though there were Executive Committee members sympathetic to André Previn, there were others who felt more or less that they ought to 'teach him a lesson' of some sort. They, unfortunately, were the dominant ones, and we, unfortunately, are the losers. If this group of high-powered CEOs thought they could run a symphony the way they run a diversified steel conglomerate, they have been proven wrong. There are some observers – such as yours truly – who feel that for bungling the Previn matter, they ought to resign. At the very least, they and manager Marshall Turkin ought to

214

stop trying to sell us the bogus line that they were the responsible fiscal watchdogs who had to 'draw the line' against a spendthrift musical director.

The fact is, the decline and fall of André Previn as conductor of the Pittsburgh Symphony was horrifying in its implications for the city's cultural life.

What most astonishes me is how a multi-talented international superstar went so quickly from toast of the town to persona non grata.

Only a small part of the answer lay in Previn's supposedly 'aloof' personality. Previn was 'aloof' the way Bobby Kennedy was 'ruthless' – because it was easy for the basically lazy local news media to perceive and label him as such, rather than to take the time and energy to figure him out. He was perceived as a snob for not socializing with the locals. . .

But the real question still remains: Did Pittsburgh's single biggest cultural light choose to leave the area or was he booted out by an executive board that – like the city itself – never fully appreciated what a catch he was in the first place?

The PSO got Previn at a time when he was making the final transition from popular to symphonic musician. We got his name, his talent, his national TV series, his international connections and reputation, and he got the major American orchestra he needed to legitimize himself, once and for all. For Pittsburgh, it was an unprecedented musical and public relations coup. His years here removed any remaining doubts as to Previn's seriousness as a classical musician. Isaac Stern called him 'one of the most underrated great conductors in the world'.

But the glitch was that Previn didn't cover his political bases, most of all his own board of directors' Executive Committee, which unwittingly (and dim-wittedly) had to choose between its music director - Previn the world-class superstar – and its obscure, prosaic symphony manager, Marshall Turkin.

So in the best interests of the PSO and the city of Pittsburgh, which of the two did the PSO Executive Committee elect to keep? Turkin.

Thanks, guys. Great choice.

You'd think at a time when the whole community is trying to stave off a general decline – the fading steel business, declining population, the departure of Gulf, turmoil and money problems in a variety of cultural institutions – the movers and shakers might have lifted more than a finger to protect what human resources we do have.

André Previn was at the top of the list of such resources. The city and the symphony will continue to exist without him; but Previn's departure was both untimely and unnecessary, and there's a shoddy, vindictive quality to the way in which it took place. Previn isolated himself to some extent from the general public. But what is puzzling and sad is the smugness with which symphony officials view his exit – as though it were good riddance to someone who'd done something wrong! As though Previn's equal or better were easy to find and the prospect of a three-to-four year search for a successor were going to be a piece of cake.

The PSO is a private organization, but with a public obligation, and it is time to take a hard look at whom it appoints to its executive board. Corporate officials are presumed to have fund-raising capabilities, but we have seen in the Previn affair that they lack both the ability and the sophistication to handle top-of-the-line conductors, not to mention aesthetic judgment in matters musical.

Previn did more for Pittsburgh – its artistic standing in America, its image, its quality of life – than all the businessmen who ultimately decided his fate. As for that recent decline in audiences [Previn was blamed for a drop in subscription sales], it couldn't possibly have anything to do with the economic woes of the area in general, could it?

If you detect a note – no, a whole symphony – of resentment toward those who let Previn slip through our fingers, it's in the hope that public attention and more intelligent media scrutiny might be applied to symphony matters in the future. This amounts to locking the Heinz Hall door after the conductor has escaped, of course.

And one more thing – something André Previn never heard here during those last ugly days of his tenure: a vote of gratitude for his talent, his industry, his excellence.

After Previn's meeting with Carl Apone, he had lunch with Jim Cunningham, a programmer and announcer for WQED-FM, and then was interviewed by Cunningham for a final farewell broadcast.

Cunningham asked Previn how he felt, preparing to leave the city, and Previn said, 'I feel a combination of very tired and very sorry. Though the festival and tour were hard, the nervous stress of the circumstances surrounding my leaving took their toll. I'm more tired than I can remember ever being in my entire life. I have one week of work with the LSO, and after that I want to recuperate. I want to lie around the garden, play with the baby, and not shave.'

Cunningham asked, 'Is there some chance we'll see you as a guest conductor somewhere down the road?' and Previn said, 'Not as a guest conductor, because the contract with Los Angeles is exclusive, in terms of American orchestras.' (There is one exception – the Boston Symphony Orchestra at Tanglewood.)

Cunningham said that a lot of people listening to the interview would always wonder why Previn left Pittsburgh, and Previn said, 'Allow me a reasonably long answer: if there were one specific person – Villain X – I wouldn't hesitate to name him, but there isn't. With the best of intentions, I couldn't pinpoint blame on anybody, so that makes it much more difficult. I certainly didn't leave

217

because the Los Angeles Orchestra has a higher profile. But I did have a very long period of disagreement not so much with the artistic goals but with the methods of how to achieve them. Those differences of opinion got to a point where somebody had to win or lose. You win one, you lose one. There was nothing I could do about that.'

Cunningham said, 'You really did want to stay in Pittsburgh', and Previn said, 'I certainly did. I had high hopes. But on the other hand, I have to look on the positive side. The die is cast. There's no getting around the fact that the Los Angeles is a great orchestra and I look forward to working with them. They have a management and a board and a city that are unbelievably behind them – in the orchestra's corner – and they seem to take any kind of risks or gambles to promote the orchestra's welfare. And that's something that's hard to resist. Once the choice was made here – mind you, not only by the people who run the orchestra but also by me – I have to look forward to this new environment as accomplishing some of the things that I *still* say could be accomplished here but weren't.'

Cunningham said, 'It's sad to say that it takes losing something before you realise how much it means to you. I can't tell you how very, very sorry I am to see you go.'

When Previn arrived in Pittsburgh, there was much fanfare. Huge billboards with 'PREVIN!' along the highways announced his presence in the city, and one resident now said, 'They never appreciated what they had. They wanted glamour, and they thought he would give it to them. They couldn't understand why he wouldn't come to parties. Solti and Giulini and Ozawa don't go to parties. Steinberg didn't go to parties. Occasionally his wife would entertain, just to quell the rumours. They never understood how hard Previn worked. They never realised he's a great artist, and you just don't jerk a great artist around like that. Now I suppose they think they can just go out and buy another one.'

Cunningham later told me, 'I saw him drive off, all alone. I just couldn't believe he was really leaving.'

CBS ran the 'Crossroads' programme with the segment on Previn early in September, and the *New York Times* television listing of the programme called Previn the 'Music Director of the Los Angeles Philharmonic'. Although there were many shots of Previn conducting the Pittsburgh Symphony, the orchestra was not identified, and in Bill Moyers' introduction he said that Previn had come full circle. And the correspondent Andrew Lack concluded, 'It will not just be the return of the native when André Previn takes over the Los Angeles Philharmonic. After twenty years, it will be for him, if you believe in Hollywood endings, a triumph as sweet as the sound of music.'

But the sweet sound of music is not always surrounded by sweetness, and Previn had not heard the last of Turkin. In September, an irate and frustrated and angry Ernest Fleischmann reported that, in a surprise move, the Pittsburgh Symphony Orchestra had been given a new contract that would put them ahead of the Los Angeles in pay scales. Fleischmann told me, 'We don't *play* catch-up anymore. And orchestra managers know what other managers are doing. I called Marshall and asked what in hell was going on, and he just said, "Orchestra morale was low, because we lost André, so we had to do something to make it up to them." ' Fleischmann is proud of the fact that he has never had a strike in Los Angeles, and now he had to all but renegotiate the musicians' contracts.

And in Pittsburgh money alone would not lift morale. In the Spitzer article, Turkin said that Previn never fired anyone, and suggested that he was afraid of his orchestra. (He did fire a harp player, and tried to fire three more musicians, but was stopped by the orchestra committee.) Turkin's statement left a large number of orchestra members trembling in fear for their jobs. Worse, in an interview with Apone about the new salaries, Turkin suggested that in the future the musicians might have to

219

cinch in their belts and settle for being the best provincial orchestra in the country. Previn was outraged. He said, 'For eight *years* I've been telling them that "provincial" is an adjective they must strike from their vocabulary.'

Spitzer reported that two conductors had refused the post of Pittsburgh music director because of the way Previn had been treated, and Turkin admitted that it might take four years to find someone. Still, spirits appeared to be high – at least on the fifth floor – in Heinz Hall. The '84–'85 season was being advertised as 'The Season of a Lifetime!' In the gallery of photographs of former Pittsburgh conductors Previn's picture had, beneath the photograph, '1976–1984'. Another reason Fleischmann was upset when he talked to me was that Previn had yet to be released from his '85–'86 contract, and he couldn't book any concerts in America until he was. (Previn's European manager, Jasper Parrott, commenting on what had happened in Pittsburgh, said, 'That's *one* thing that won't be in Ronald Wilford's autobiography.' But that could have been a biased comment, because, it turns out, one more thing Previn has to put up with in his busy life is the fact that his two managers bicker with each other about a lot of things – including which one should have the annoying task of negotiating record contracts, and one time, in exasperation, they left to Turkin the task of figuring the division of royalties, when any orchestra member could have told them that Turkin's grasp of the contracts he had drawn up was so minimal that the orchestra lost at least one recording while he tried to figure out the financial details. So much for cost accounting and counterpoint.)

Previn had one more orchestra to say goodbye to forever: the LSO. Actually, it was a combination of a farewell and a celebration, the celebration being the orchestra's eightieth anniversary. He conducted an all-Elgar programme, and the reviews were also a welcome home:

In the *Guardian*, Michael John White wrote, in part,

This 80th birthday concert by the LSO floated on a buoyant mood of self-congratulation. . . with the LSO hyped up to prove it can, given a fair wind and the right man on the rostrum, play with the strength, style and energy of a great orchestra. The right man here was André Previn, making his last appearance as the LSO's Conductor Emeritus. . . He handles the stubborn Englishness of turn-of-the-century Elgar as brilliantly as he attunes to the more visionary English pastoral of Vaughan Williams or the spidery English wit of Walton – and in each case with a sense of theatre and (I hesitate to say it) glamour that you wouldn't necessarily expect to find on reading the composers' scores. . .

In the *Daily Telegraph*, Anthony Payne wrote, in part,

. . .Mr. Previn has proved to be barely equalled in our native repertory, and has shown the most moving insights into such as Walton, Vaughan Williams, and Elgar. In fact, the climax of the evening was reached with a really superb performance of the 'Enigma Variations', beautifully paced and rhythmically sprung, in which Nimrod made a quite overwhelming impact at the centre of the structure and the composer himself closed the formal arch with wonderful lyric solemnity and impetuosity.

The numerous exquisite moments of private emotion expressed in Elgar's chamber music-like scoring were also most poetically characterised, and one felt happy to be listening to an orchestra and conductor so at one with themselves and the music. . .

The concert ended with an encore, and the first 'Pomp and Circumstance' march, performed with immense élan and pride, and one thought as Mr. Previn was recalled again and again that no one deserved his applause better.

Previn spent two weeks with his children in Connecticut, but for the first time in many years he skipped Tanglewood entirely. Back in Surrey he rested and recuperated and when he was finally feeling energy return he finished the piano concerto for Ashkenazy. He said, 'It's *fiendishly* difficult. I made it as tough as I possibly could, but the son of a bitch will probably read right through it.' To celebrate the completion of the piece he said he'd bought an Augustus John. (Of his art collection he says, 'Most of the paintings and drawings in my collection were bought a long time ago, before you had to be Paul Getty to buy even a scrawl by a newcomer. Over the years, I have said goodbye to works by Balthus, Léger, O'Keeffe, Hartley, Dove, Sloan, Henri, Nolde and others, but I've gradually begun to acquire pieces of art that I like.)

In Surrey, the dining room had been completed, the piano concerto pronounced a success (Ashkenazy told Previn he hoped to perform it all over the world), and Previn was making daily trips to the National Theatre, where a new Tom Stoppard play was in rehearsal. Previn had contributed five songs, for which Stoppard wrote the lyrics.

Previn was really excited about his first concerts with the Royal Philharmonic Orchestra: the André Previn Music Festival, in the Royal Festival Hall, June 16th through the 30th. He would have some of his favourite soloists: in addition to Ashkenazy, Pinchas Zukerman, Yo-Yo Ma, Isaac Stern, and Dame Janet Baker. He would conduct the London premiere of John Harbison's 'Ulysses' Bow'; two performances of his beloved Brahms *Requiem*; the Ravel opera *L'Heure Espagnole*, with Jessye Norman; Messiaen's 'Et Exspecto Resurrectionem Mortuorum'. An as yet untitled piece of Previn's would be performed by the Philip Jones Brass Ensemble. There would be orchestra works by Mozart, Walton, more Ravel ('Daphnis and Chloe' – complete), Rachmaninoff, Mahler, Elgar, Richard Strauss. For those who would enjoy a change of pace, there would be an evening of film classics with Henry

Mancini; Buddy Rich and his Orchestra; Ella Fitzgerald and Friends; Oscar Peterson and Friends.

Previn called from Surrey. He said, 'Chubbs is *walking*. He takes five or six steps, and then falls over. And he's so proud of himself. He walks, and then he falls down, and then he makes this very Italian gesture of self-approval. He puts his hand over his heart and smiles. It's wonderful. He's a terrific little friend.'

In early October, Previn, together with Heather and the baby, flew over the Pole to Los Angeles to look for a house and get acquainted with the orchestra. Previn was amazed at the largesse in Los Angeles. He would have, in addition to the normal orchestra schedule, a modern-music series; a chamber-music series; a summer school for young musicians (the Institute of the Los Angeles Philharmonic, founded by Fleischmann, with Leonard Bernstein as the first music director); money for recordings and first-rank guest conductors. Most important, he would have a managing director who loved music and musicians, and who would work with him and not against him. Previn had, at first, thought of the change as a sidestep, but then he was flooded with congratulatory wires from fellow-musicians on his new post. The Previns returned to Surrey by way of Pittsburgh, where, on 16 October, Previn gave a fund-raising concert with Ella Fitzgerald and raised seventy-five thousand dollars for the Rehabilitation Center.

In November, Previn was finally freed from his Pittsburgh contract, and a jubilant Fleischmann announced to the press that Previn would open the Los Angeles Philharmonic's 1985–86 season. Fleischmann had been raising funds and making plans for a number of television programmes, and he hired Stephen Dick to produce them and also lured Dinah Daniels away from the Met to come to Los Angeles and head the orchestra's marketing department. The two had always worked well with Previn, and he would surely be off to a good start with his new orchestra. He could even be entering what Norman

Lebrecht, of the London *Times*, might agree is his fifth period, for, as more than one of his friends have observed, there are no obstacles for Previn.

INDEX